Sunderland

City and People Since 1945

Sunderland
City and People Since 1945

Neil T. Sinclair

Sunderland Echo

breedon **books**
PUBLISHING

First published in Great Britain in 2004 by
The Breedon Books Publishing Company Limited
Breedon House, 3 The Parker Centre,
Derby, DE21 4SZ.

ISBN 1 85983 404 3

Printed and bound by Butler & Tanner,
Frome, Somerset, England.

Cover printing by Lawrence-Allen Colour Printers,
Weston-super-Mare, Somerset, England.

Contents

Foreword

All towns change, but Sunderland has had change thrust upon it. The townsfolk in 1945 would have looked from Wearmouth Bridge at the noisy riverbanks, crowded with cranes and ship-building sheds and coal-staiths and loomed over by a huge pit-wheel, and thought: this is what we're all about – and always will be.

In the new millennium, a visitor strolling over the bridge would hardly guess at what has been swept away: below are the buildings of the University campus; there's a neat riverside walk, there's a football stadium atop the pit, there is little that hints at the past.

I find it odd that this has happened in my lifetime, that the town into which my roots burrowed has faded into a Victorian picture, a history of heavy industry. And I have to accept that all this change has been wrought from outside, with little consultation to comfort the men and women who worked in the yards and glassworks and at the coal-face.

Nevertheless, there's an unseen history which has to provide the basis for the future: the sense of being part of a huge village, of having come through tough times, and having to adapt and survive.

Coming from Wearside is still something to be proud of. I've been fortunate in my work to travel the world. I can't count the times when my home town is mentioned when thousands of miles away. A mutual connection to Sunderland is seized on, a quick scamper through 'been to see the Lads recently? Fawcett Street's never been the same since the Town Hall disappeared, and what is that thing on the roundabout at Seaburn – a fountain or a brick gasometer?' brings you close at once.

It's a city to cherish.

Kate Adie

Acknowledgements

Many people and organisations have helped me in the preparation of this book. The support of the *Sunderland Echo* has been significant and I am particularly grateful to Carol Roberton of the *Echo* who has given me much useful guidance and information as well as commenting on the text. My thanks are also due to my wife Helen and Ian Carr for reading through the text.

I would like to thank all those who spent time in talking to me about aspects of the history of Sunderland since 1945 or answering particular queries. They include Colin Anderson, Ralph Baxter, Tim Brown, Paul Callaghan, David Cottam, Bryan Charlton, Harry and Mary Crann, Neville Curle, Norman Dennis, Brian Dodds, Jim Gardner, Peter Gibson, Forster Johnson, Frank Nicholson, John Pacey, Colin Sinclair, Charles Slater, Gordon Smith, Bob Symonds, Tom Shaw and Peter Wood.

Help has also been given by the staff of several different organisations: City Hospitals Sunderland NHS Trust, City of Sunderland Cultural and Community Services (City Library and Tourism sections), Storey Carpets, *Sunderland Echo* library, Sunderland Teaching Primary Care Trust, Edward Thompson, Tyne and Wear Museums, University of Sunderland and Reg Vardy. In my research I have consulted the files of the *Sunderland Echo* and the publications listed in the Bibliography.

The majority of the photographs are from the *Sunderland Echo*'s collection and I am grateful to Doreen Talbot, photographic librarian, for her assistance in locating and printing these illustrations. Thanks are also due to Ian Carr and George Edwards for providing photographs they took in the past, to Martin Routledge for help with photographs from the Sunderland Museum and Winter Gardens (Tyne and Wear Museums) collection, to Anthony Kerr of the University of Sunderland and to all others who have helped with supplying prints.

The illustrations are by courtesy of the *Sunderland Echo* apart from the following pages: Author/Author's collection 64, 67, 68 bottom, 77, 79, 81 bottom, 82 bottom, 84 bottom, 85 bottom, 89 bottom, 91, 94, 95, 97, 129 top, 133 bottom, 137, 138, 139 bottom, 141, 142 bottom, 143 bottom, 144 top, 146 bottom, 149 bottom; G.C. Bartam 103; Ian S. Carr 50, 55 top, 56 middle, 62 bottom, 73, 85 top, 96 top and bottom, 117, 133 top, 134, 152 top; Cottam Brothers 151; City of Sunderland 88, 91, 100, 145, 146 top; City Hospitals NHS Trust 119, 120, 149 top; Neville Curle 51, 53, 54; George Edwards 24, 39 bottom, 41 top, 43 bottom, 60, 62 top left, 64, 74, 75, 82 top and middle, 94, 95, 123 bottom, 133 bottom, 137, 138, 140, 142 bottom, 143 top; Roy Elwen 132 bottom; Peter Gibson 66 middle and bottom; Leighton 153, Sir Paul Nicholson 105; Sybil Reeder 132 top; Storey Carpets 109; Tom Soulsby 123 top; Sunderland Museum and Winter Gardens (Tyne and Wear Museums) 12, 14 bottom, 16, 23 middle, 25, 29, 37, 40 bottom, 55, 83, 87, 112, 128; Sunderland, Marine Activities Centre/Tyne and Wear Development Corporation 92; Edward Thompson 58; Keith Turnbull 81 top; University of Sunderland 7, 43 top, 98, 99, 107 bottom.

Introduction

When I came to work in Sunderland in 1972 I knew that the town was nationally known for shipbuilding, coalmining and Pyrex glassware. Having lived in Scotland, I was also aware that Sunderland was the headquarters of Binns, the department store which had a shop in Edinburgh, and of Vaux the brewers who owned Usher's brewery and pubs as well as the Swallow Hotels north of the Border.

Thirty years later, when I retired as Senior Curator of Sunderland Museums in 2002, all these pillars of life on Wearside, with the sole exception of Pyrex, had, almost unbelievably, disappeared. In their place were several new kinds of employment. This book charts these massive changes that have taken place in Sunderland. It also looks at topics such as local government, health, housing, education, transport and leisure and the leading business people and politicians.

Sunderland's boundaries expanded during the second half of the 20th century and I have tried to cover the districts which were part of the local authority during the period of the different chapters. There is, however, generally more detail about the area of the County Borough which existed in 1945.

I have attempted to discuss the main aspects of Sunderland since 1945, but am conscious that coverage of certain subjects has necessarily been brief. The Bibliography at the end of the book lists publications which look in more detail at some of these topics.

I hope that *Sunderland – City and People Since 1945* contributes to a wider appreciation of the history of the city and its people in the 60 years since the end of World War Two.

Neil Sinclair
Sunderland
December 2003

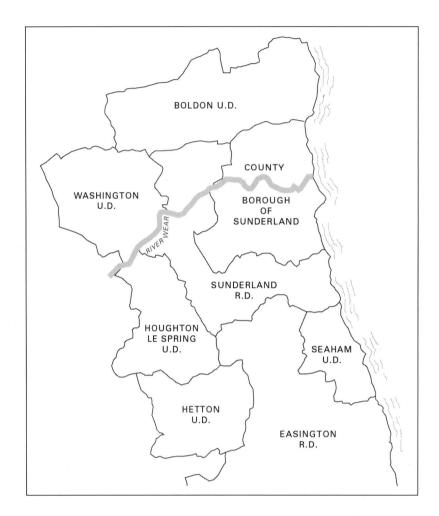

The County Borough of Sunderland and the surrounding Rural District (R.D.) and Urban District (U.D.) Councils in 1945. In 1951 the County Borough, which had extended up to its boundaries, took over parts of the Rural District. In 1967 the whole of the remaining Rural District and the South Bents area of Boldon Urban District were absorbed. The new Borough of Sunderland, created in 1974, included the County Borough and Hetton, Houghton-le-Spring and Washington Urban Districts and the Burdon and Warden Law parishes of Easington District.

CHAPTER I

The Largest Shipbuilding Town in the World

The River Wear

The best impression of Sunderland in 1945 would have been gained by looking east down the Wear from the Wearmouth Bridge. The banks of the river were dominated by shipbuilding – shipyards, repair yards, fitting out quays and marine engine works.

Sunderland, as Wearsiders were proud to point out, was 'the largest shipbuilding town in the world'. In the six years from the outbreak of

The view east from Wearmouth Bridge during World War Two showing a hive of shipbuilding and ship repairing activity. In the foreground is Austin's yard with a ship under repair on the pontoon on the left. In the centre of the Wear is a barrage balloon, part of the defences against German bombers, and beyond on the north bank a ship is being fitted out at Dickinson's Marine Engine Works. A camouflaged vessel is being completed at J.L. Thompson's outfitting yard.

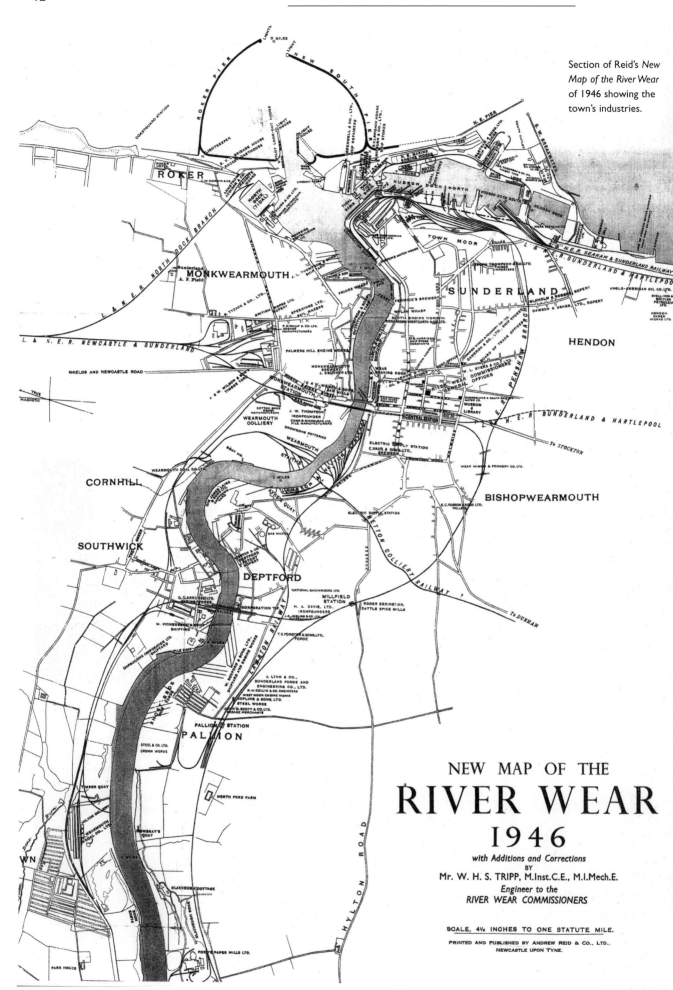

Section of Reid's *New Map of the River Wear* of 1946 showing the town's industries.

World War Two in September 1939, 245 merchant ships totalling almost 1,502,000 tons were built on the Wear, 27 percent of the entire output of all the yards in the United Kingdom. The total excluded the naval vessels also built in Sunderland.

The Wear had played another important role in wartime shipbuilding. J.L. Thompson, whose outfitting yard could be seen on the north or Monkwearmouth bank of the river, had developed the prototype of the American Liberty Ship standard cargo vessel. This was to be one of the most significant ship designs of the 1940s.

The Wear was still in many ways the lifeblood of the town. In addition to shipbuilding it was the reason why so many industries had grown up along its banks and why Sunderland had become a major port, particularly for shipping coal. The entrance to the South Docks, opened in 1850 and extended in 1868, lay beyond the curve of the Wear. Just visible, however, was Corporation Quay, a deep-water facility on the riverbank opened in 1934.

Corporation Quay had been financed by Sunderland Council, but was engineered and managed by the River Wear Commission. The Commission had been established in 1717 to improve the river. In the next 80 years it built the south and north inner piers and from the 1880s to the 1900s constructed the vast outer piers. The Commission deepened and widened the Wear and it also took over the South Docks and the relatively unsuccessful North Dock of 1837, both of which had been built by private companies. The South Docks had flourished, particularly for shipping coal. Around the edges of the Docks were industries such as shipbuilding, timber yards and chemical works.

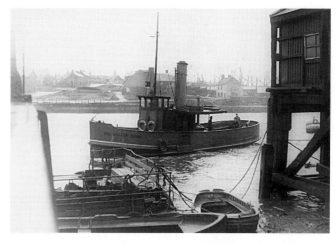

The *Sir Walter Raine* passenger ferry arriving at the East End landing stage from Monkwearmouth. The ferry, which had continued to charge a halfpenny fare from the 18th century, carried workers across the Wear. It closed in 1957 after the demolition of houses on the riverside, such as those in the background, had reduced the number of passengers.

Maritime industries dominated the banks of the river, but houses for the workers in these industries were also in evidence. The older houses on the river banks had been demolished to make way for industrial expansion and because many of them had become overcrowded slums.

On the opposite side of the Wearmouth Bridge coal, the other major industry on Wearside, was much in evidence in the view to the west. Coal mining was the reason for the existence of most of the villages and towns surrounding Sunderland and Wearmouth Colliery, on the north bank of the Wear, was close to the heart of the town.

Corporation Quay, soon after completion in 1934, with tugs waiting to take ships between the river and the sea standing below the 'bunkering' conveyor for coaling ships. Beyond a ship is awaiting loading at the deep-water quay. In the background are the houses of the East End which once came right down to the river bank.

Aerial view, looking north, of the harbour entrance showing the two inner piers with the outer south pier in the foreground. The river entrance to the Docks is on the left. To the north of the inner piers are Monkwearmouth and Roker.

On the south bank the coal industry had produced the Lambton and Hetton Staiths which stretched for half a mile up the river. Here the coal which had been brought by the Lambton, Hetton and Joicey Company's railways from their pits further inland was transferred to the sea-going collier ships which sailed to London and other destinations on the east coast of Britain.

At the top of the cliffs above the Lambton and Hetton Staiths were Vaux Brewery, one of the town's best-known commercial names, and Sunderland Corporation Electricity Works, powered by coal brought by the colliery railways. Attached to the electricity works were the Corporation Transport's tramway depot and works.

Beyond the Staiths was Deptford. Two of the major firms in this area were Sir James Laing's shipyard and Webster's Ropery. Webster's was the world's earliest factory for machine-made rope and opened in 1795. There were several other rope-making firms in the town; their growth had been encouraged by the shipbuilding industry.

Deptford and adjoining Millfield had once been the home of several major glassworks. The sole survivor was James A. Jobling, whose works lay a quarter of a mile inland. Their Pyrex glassware, albeit reduced to 'utility' designs, was one of the country's most popular household products.

Around the bend in the river from Pallion the Queen Alexandra Bridge dominated the Wear. It had been built in 1909 to provide a road and rail link between the districts of Pallion and Southwick (independent of

The Corporation tram depot (front) and electricity works run diagonally across this aerial view of Deptford. To the right and left of the electricity works are the Hetton Staiths, with the Wearmouth Colliery Staiths on the opposite side of the river. Single-storey cottages dominate the housing on the left.

Low Southwick showing (bottom left) the Queen Alexandra Bridge, which linked Southwick to Pallion in the 1930s. Opened in 1909, the bottom level carried the road, while the upper deck was for railway use, although this ceased by the mid-1920s. To the right of the bridge are George Clark's Engine Works.

Sunderland County Borough until 1928). Below the bridge were two of the major maritime industries in the town – Doxford's marine engine works and shipyard in Pallion and Pickersgill's yard in Southwick.

The industrial area of the river stopped just beyond the County Borough boundaries at Pallion and Southwick with Hylton Colliery in Castletown on the north bank and Ford Paper Works in South Hylton. This had been the first works in the country to produce paper from esparto grass on a large scale.

At Pallion new industry, such as Steel's, whose products included Coles cranes, was developing in industrial estates away from the river banks. Industry had been

Pallion with a mass of railway tracks. From the 1850s new industry, such as Forster's Forge in the centre, tended to be sited near the railways rather than the river. The wagons on the left contain steel for Doxford's shipyard.

moving away from the Wear since the growth of the railway system in the second half of the 19th century. The process had accelerated with increasing reliance on road transport, but the industries which were based on the Wear – shipbuilding and coal shipment – seemed certain to be the basis of Sunderland's prosperity for many years to come.

The Town Centre, East End and Monkwearmouth

The Borough of Sunderland was created in 1835 from the townships of Monkwearmouth, on the north bank of the river, and Bishopwearmouth and Sunderland on the south. While Monkwearmouth had retained its identity, Bishopwearmouth had become the town centre and Sunderland parish, at the mouth of the Wear, was now known as the East End.

The main arteries in the town centre were High Street West and Bridge and Fawcett Streets. High Street had developed to link the settlements of Sunderland and Bishopwearmouth. Bridge and Fawcett Streets were two of the roads which had been built to link the original Wearmouth Bridge of 1796 ('the largest cast-iron bridge in the world') with the routes to Newcastle and South Shields in the north and to Stockton in the south.

The Wearmouth road (right) and railway bridges carry the transport links from the north over the Wear; Bridge Street leads south from the road bridge. Timber for Wilson's sawmill can be seen in the river to the right of the bridges. The tower of the Central Station can be seen in the bottom right of this 1930s view and the white façade of the newly-extended Marks & Spencer in the bottom left of this pre-war photograph.

The next major transport development had been the Wearmouth Junction Railway of 1879 with the railway bridge (in its turn 'the largest hog-back iron girder bridge in the world') over the river and the new

The Echo office in Bridge Street during World War Two. The *Sunderland Echo*, established in 1873, was the town's evening paper, widely read throughout the area. Its Conservative politics reflected those of the owning Storey family.

Bridge Street with St Mary's Catholic Church on the right. The corner of the ornate Elephant Tea House can be seen in the distance with the tower of the Town Hall in Fawcett Street just visible beyond. Bridge and Fawcett Streets carried through traffic from Newcastle and South Shields to Stockton.

Sunderland Central Station. The rather gloomy station was situated below street level with the main entrance below a large, but undistinguished, tower in High Street West.

High Street West had a wide range of shops. These included old-established Sunderland firms, such as Jopling's and Blackett's, and branches of national chains including Marks & Spencer and Home and Colonial Stores.

Beyond the main shopping

The 'Hot Potato Man' in his regular stance outside the Theatre Royal Cinema in Bedford Street. One of the town's best-known characters, he was fondly remembered by many Wearsiders and still appears in paintings and prints produced today.

The 'Crab Lady' who sold fresh-boiled crabs from the north end of Sunderland Central Station.

area in High Street West there were several public buildings. These included the swimming baths, and the magistrates courts, police and fire stations and the Empire Theatre. The last four, along with the impressive Empire Theatre, were all designed by the notable Sunderland architects W. & T.R. Milburn and were built in the 1900s when Sunderland's years of prosperity had not yet ended.

High Street West looking towards the junction with Fawcett Street. Shops predominate, although two pubs can also be seen. Kennedy's, like Blackett's further along the street, was one of the smaller department stores.

The bombed site of the Empress Hotel and Jacky White's Market, operating in the open since its building was destroyed by bombing. The market still thrives in the 2000s, under cover again, in this area. In spite of the notice, the Empress Hotel was never rebuilt. Phoenix Buildings are in the right background. The site was later used for a temporary bus station.

The last noteworthy building at the end of High Street West was St Michael's or Bishopwearmouth Church. It had been a mediaeval foundation, but the present structure dated from the 19th and 20th century.

Fawcett Street was the town's administrative and commercial centre. Towards the centre were the branches of the major banks. To the south was the Town Hall, with its much-loved clock tower. Its prominence reflected the important role of the County Borough Council in running the affairs of the town. Schools, colleges, roads, electricity and transport, council housing, parks and cemeteries, museum and library, cleansing, fire brigade and police services, as well as the municipal hospitals, were among the council's many responsibilities.

Other organisations which provided services for Sunderland people had offices near the Town Hall. These included the Sunderland Working Men's Building Society and the Sunderland Gas Company offices in Fawcett Street. In adjacent streets were the River Wear Commissioners, the Sunderland & South Shields Water Company and the London & North Eastern Railway district offices. John Street and the streets to the west contained the smaller offices of solicitors, accountants and other professions.

On both sides at the south end of Fawcett Street were empty spaces where the two main blocks of Binns, Sunderland's major department store, had stood until destroyed by bombing in 1941. It had then relocated to several other premises in the town centre. Binns was of regional importance and had branches in the north east of England and Scotland. The large size of their Sunderland store was because the town was the major shopping centre for the eastern part of County Durham.

The derelict land where Binns had once stood was a reminder that Sunderland had been among the seven most badly bombed towns and cities in the country as German planes had sought to destroy the shipyards. In the town centre bombing had also destroyed part of the roof of the Central Station, the Empress Hotel, St Thomas's Church, the Winter Gardens at the back of the Library and Museum and the Victoria Hall, the major centre for public meetings and entertainment.

The boundary of the town centre was

Fawcett Street looking north from the junction with Borough Road in about 1949. The Town Hall of 1890 dominates the scene. The bombed site of Binns stores can be seen on either side of the road. Beyond on the right is another Binns building (now the entrance block of the City Library).

marked by Mowbray Park. On its northern edge was the Central Library and Museum. It was Sunderland's first major municipal building when erected in 1879 and marked the growing economic confidence of the town. Conversely the fact that a planned and much-needed extension had not been built in the 1930s reflected the economic depression then affecting Sunderland.

The prosperity of the town centre contrasted with the run-down East End. The surviving, but decaying, Georgian houses and the former Exchange Building, as well as the Anglican Churches of Holy Trinity and St John's, showed that the area around the

John Street which was one of a group of residential streets built in the 1830s in what later became the town centre. Fawcett Street had largely been rebuilt from the 1870s, but John and Frederick Streets were little changed although the buildings were now all used for solicitors' and other offices.

port had once been a very prosperous one. From the beginning of the 19th century, however, the middle classes moved to Bishopwearmouth and the houses became over-crowded slums.

St Peter's, Monkwearmouth, was Sunderland's most historic building. The Saxon tower still remained, but the rest of the church had been rebuilt.

The bad housing had resulted in Harrison's Buildings, Sunderland's first council houses, being built in this area in 1903. They had been followed by the Garths in 1937 which, along with some other public housing developments, were built by the North East Housing Association; both these houses and those built by the Corporation were generally known as 'council houses'. The inhabitants of many of the houses cleared as part of the slum clearance programme before the war had, however, been moved to the new council estates on the edge of the town.

The Garths were one of the major public housing developments of the inter-war years. Unlike the other council houses built on greenfield sites, they were flats. In the background are the old East End houses, due for demolition.

Monkwearmouth, on the north bank of the Wear, was the third and oldest of the townships which made up the original Borough of Sunderland in 1835. It had developed around the Saxon Monastery of St Peter's, where the Venerable Bede had been a

monk. The church still survived, but was hemmed in by later developments. The whole surrounding part of Monkwearmouth consisted of poor quality overcrowded housing.

The main street of Monkwearmouth was North Bridge Street, which connected the road from Newcastle to the iron bridge. It had some fine architecture, particularly the classical station built by George Hudson, the 'Railway King' and Sunderland's MP, as the terminus of the railway from Newcastle. To the west of the railway lay Wearmouth Colliery and the surrounding pitmen's houses. The colliery area of Monkwearmouth merged into Southwick.

Sunderland's Suburbs and Surrounding Villages

During the Victorian period Sunderland experienced a population explosion. North of the river Monkwearmouth expanded. South of the Wear the new working-class suburbs of Millfield, Pallion and Hendon grew up close to new industries such as glass, paper rope and iron works. Much of the housing in these areas was provided by the single-storey cottages which were found in Sunderland in far greater numbers than any other large town in the country.

Ashbrooke, to the south of Mowbray Park, became the prime residential area of Sunderland in the 19th century. The grounds of a few large houses, which had been built by the leading Victorian commercial and industrial personalities, were surrounded by terraces of two and three-storey houses. Some of these were in private streets with gates at either end.

Two of the largest houses in the area were now used for higher education – Ashburne by the Art College and Langham Tower as the Training College for teachers. Together with the Technical College in Green Terrace they were administered by the Corporation.

A Sunderland cottage in Westbury Street, one of many streets of cottages in the Millfield area. This cottage still has its original two-leaf outer door.

Ashbrooke also had a fine skyline with the towers and spires of Anglican Christ Church, Methodist St John's and Park Road, Presbyterian St George's and Congregational West Park. Several of these churches had followed their congregations as they moved westwards in the 1880s and 1890s, leaving the dwindling number of churchgoers in the East End to be served by mission churches.

Unlike the working-class areas of the town Ashbrooke had few shops; shopping was delivered by the traders or collected by the servants. Its middle-class status was reflected not only by the number of churches, but also by Ashbrooke sports ground, the centre for sports such as cricket, rugby, tennis and bowls.

Less grand middle-class housing than in Ashbrooke had been provided from the 1900s in the High Barnes area close to Chester Road. Here they were close to institutions which had been deliberately built on the edge of the town in the mid-19th century – Bishopwearmouth Cemetery and the former Sunderland Union Workhouse. The latter had now become the Municipal Hospital and Highfield Institute.

The majority of the new middle-class housing before 1914 had been south of the Wear, although development had taken place in Roker close to the seafront which was growing into the village of Fulwell. An outstanding building in this area was St Andrew's Church at Roker of 1907, the 'Cathedral of the Arts and Crafts Movement'. The area also housed Roker Park, home of Sunderland Football Club since 1898; the club had several years of success in the years before 1939, including winning the FA Cup in 1937.

The years between the wars saw a significant expansion in Sunderland's suburbs. The area available to build new houses was increased by the

The view south-west from Tunstall Hills towards Ashbrooke in 1937; the stand of the sports club is on the left. Two and three-storey houses predominate; the cottages and industry lie closer to the river and the sea. The spires of several Sunderland churches and the Town Hall tower (centre) can be seen on the skyline.

The Municipal Hospital and the Highfield Institute buildings (the former Sunderland Union Workhouse), dominate this view taken in the 1930s. Kayll Road runs across the foreground. There is a mix of 1930s semi-detached and two-storey and cottage terraced housing.

incorporation of Fulwell and Southwick Urban District Councils into the County Borough in 1928.

The types of new housing in the absorbed areas reflected the different nature of the Urban Districts. In Fulwell large numbers of private houses were built at Seaburn, while in Southwick the Marley Pots, High Southwick and Carley Hill council estates were built.

The 1920s and 1930s private housing south of the Wear was mainly in the Grangetown District and the area close to Queen Alexandra Road, the new ring road. The council house development in the southern suburbs was concentrated in the Ford and Humbledon Estates.

These new private houses were almost all semi-detached or bungalows. They occupied larger ground areas than their predecessors as all had their front and back gardens. The pre-World War One houses had backyards and, at best, very small front gardens.

Several of the town's institutions had been re-sited in the new suburbs. Bede Girls' and Boys' Collegiate Schools moved to Humbledon, the Eye Infirmary to Queen Alexandra Road and Monkwearmouth Hospital to Fulwell.

The growth of Seaburn as one of Sunderland's 'twin seaside resorts' (alongside Roker) was another feature of the 1930s. The illuminations, the Seaburn Hall for concerts and dances, the fairground, the Seaburn Hotel, shops and cafés were all features of this development. The seashore at Roker and Seaburn often surprised visitors to the town, who invariably commented favourably on it.

The Sunderland Rural District Council area lay immediately outside the boundaries of the County Borough. While much of the area was still farmland it also included three colliery villages – Ryhope, Silksworth and Castletown. Pit villages had their own distinctive identities. The Co-operative stores were the biggest shops and the Ryhope and Silksworth Industrial and Provident Society provided many of the services of a department store as well as food and funerals.

The other villages in the Rural District were South Hylton, where Ford

Paper Works and Forster's Forge were the main employers, and East Herrington. This was a mainly residential area on the Sunderland to Durham road which had been built up further in the 1930s.

Beyond Sunderland Rural District were the Rural District of Easington and the Urban Districts of Seaham, Houghton, Hetton, Washington and Boldon. Many of the services in these Urban Districts, as well as the Rural District, were provided by Durham County Council. Nearly all the towns and villages in these areas had again grown up around the local collieries. Most of their inhabitants looked to Sunderland as the commercial and industrial centre for East Durham.

Aerial view looking towards the beach at Roker and Seaburn in the early 1930s. Roker Park is in the top right of the photograph with St Andrew's Church in the centre. The terraces in Roker and cottages in Fulwell have been joined by more recent semi-detached houses. On the left Seaburn is being developed with bungalows under construction.

Sunderland at the end of World War Two would have been immediately recognisable to anyone who knew it at the end of the previous war in 1918. There had been some noticeable changes; on the one hand, new council and private housing estates had grown up on the outskirts, while, on the other, German bombing had left some significant gaps in the town centre.

An Industrial Working-Class Town

In 1945 Sunderland was seen as a rather unglamorous, largely working-class industrial town relying mainly on heavy industry. There were nevertheless many attractive features about Wearside. L.S. Lowry, whose works were exhibited at the museum as early as 1942,

summed up some of these when he wrote after one of his frequent stays at Seaburn in the 1960s: 'I like Sunderland because of the shipping and shipbuilding and the countryside at the back... I like the sea'.

A.A. Halsey in his introduction to Norman Dennis's *People and Planning* in 1970 picked out the same physical features as having helped to define the nature of Sunderland and its population, then gave a very incisive view of the town:

Silksworth Colliery, one of the many pits in the East Durham Coalfield. It had been sunk by the Marquis of Londonderry, but had later been sold to Lord Joicey's Lambton and Hetton Collieries.

> Sunderland, as a town, has a distinct character. It is geographically set off by its position on the river and the coast. Centred visibly and

The beach at Seaburn in the post-war years when it attracted families from many parts of Durham as well as from the town. During World War Two it was closed off.

closely on its productive work it is the antithesis of suburbia: housing is an annexe to the workplace and the community is a working community. It is, in a double sense, a working class town. Sunderland also has a social distinctiveness which is part reflection and part cause of its physical isolation. There is the shared dialect and accent of the Wearsider, local patriotism for the town's football team, the community and neighbourhood pubs and social clubs, and the collective consciousness of a harsh industrial history...

Another shared feeling among many 'Mackems' was that Sunderland suffered from having Newcastle upon Tyne only 12 miles to the north; national journalists would sometimes refer to events on Wearside taking place 'near Newcastle'. The Northumberland city was clearly the regional capital with finer architecture than Sunderland, but its inhabitants were felt to be unnecessarily superior about their status.

The sense of lack of national recognition of Sunderland was probably increased because the Wear built cargo, and not the more spectacular passenger ships. The *Mauretania* from the Tyne and the *Queen Mary* from the Clyde were well known, but not the everyday vessels from the Wear on which a significant amount of the country's trade depended.

The People of Sunderland

One significant factor affecting the nature of the people was that the Borough of Sunderland had grown massively from 25,000 in 1801 to 64,000 in 1851, 146,000 in 1901 and 185,000 in 1931 after the incorporation of Southwick and Fulwell. The growth of the population was the result of the need to find workers for the shipbuilding, coal, glass, shipping and other industries, but their decline led to a fall to 181,000 in 1951; no census was held during the war.

The vast influx of new inhabitants in the 19th century came from many parts of the British Isles, but particularly from the rural areas of the north east and, to a lesser extent, from Ireland and Scotland. Most appeared to integrate quickly into a long-established community. It was often the churches they worshipped at which showed the origins of the incomers; the Catholic church in the East End was St Patrick's and the Presbyterian

Church in North Bridge Street was known as the 'Scotch Church' in Victorian times.

There had been a small Jewish community in Sunderland since the mid-18th century which had increased significantly in the late 19th century when Jews escaping persecution from Eastern Europe arrived in the town. By the middle of the 20th century the Jewish community was playing a role in the life of the town which was greater than its numbers would have suggested. Newman Richardson was elected to the Town Council in 1915 and was to be followed by several from the community who were to play a significant part in the politics of the town. Other members were involved in commerce and the medical and legal professions. In 1953 the *Sunderland Directory* recorded an accountant, four dentists, 12 doctors and three solicitors from the Jewish community.

The arrival of the Jews from Eastern Europe was an exception to what was becoming an indigenous and settled society. Only six percent of the men in the Borough in 1901 had been born outside England and Wales. By 1961 the percentage of the population born beyond the same national

Ryhope Road alongside Backhouse Park at the edge of Ashbrooke. The spire of Christ Church is in the background and the synagogue opened in 1928 on the right. Many members of the town's influential Jewish community lived in the area and a Talmudical College for training rabbis was later established nearby.

boundaries had fallen to 2.4 percent, lower than any other comparable town.

Within Sunderland people tended to associate themselves with the particular part of the town they lived in. There was a division between north and south of the river; if you lived in the north you would think twice before moving south of the Wear. The East Enders who had to move to council houses in the Southwick area before the war used to go back to shops and pubs in their former home area. The villages around the town certainly regarded themselves as distinct from Sunderland. Two, South Hylton and Whitburn, even had their own bus companies, Jolly and Economic, based there, something that had become unusual in urban areas in the 1940s.

The majority of Sunderland people would have described themselves as working class. This term covered a wide range of people from the skilled shipyard artisans living in the cottages they owned in Millfield to the families who had suffered from unemployment in the 1930s living in the overcrowded houses with poor services in the East End.

The assumption of many of the working-class families was that son would follow father into the same industry. This was particularly the case in shipbuilding where preference was given to sons of workers. It was

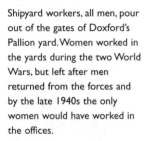

Shipyard workers, all men, pour out of the gates of Doxford's Pallion yard. Women worked in the yards during the two World Wars, but left after men returned from the forces and by the late 1940s the only women would have worked in the offices.

The Old Market in
High Street East in
the 1930s. It was
situated in the East
End where there was
much poverty and the
second-hand clothes on sale
would have been all that some
could afford.

certainly not always true as, for instance, many miners saw education as a means for their sons to avoid an industry they did not wish them to enter. Bede, Monkwearmouth and Ryhope Grammar Schools undoubtedly provided a way out for bright working-class children. The probability of son following father into the shipyards and other industries was, however, a disincentive for some to progress beyond the school leaving age and Sunderland was to have a continuing problem in the number of its people who had no educational qualifications.

The emphasis on the career of the sons reflected the male bias of much of working-class society. One example of this is the tradition of the men going to the pub or club at midday on Sundays and arriving home to have their lunches placed on the table before them. It should not, however, be implied that the visit to the pub or club was by any means universal, as there was still a strong Nonconformist, particularly Methodist, tradition linked to teetotalism in the town.

The middle class in Sunderland was proportionally smaller than in most towns of a similar size. It had a particularly small upper middle class as many of the leading shipbuilding and other industrial families had moved to the larger houses in Whitburn, Cleadon or in the countryside around Durham City. Even though the industrialists came to work in the town they almost certainly felt less involvement than if they lived there.

The middle class who did live in Sunderland tended to be the smaller business and professional people such as the shipyard managers, bankers, college lecturers, solicitors and doctors. They formed the nucleus of the local societies, such as the Antiquarians, and the membership of the churches in the Ashbrooke and Roker areas. They expected their children to go to Bede or Monkwearmouth Grammar Schools, or to the fee-paying Argyle House or Tonstall Schools or Sunderland High School in the case of girls.

Kate Adie, a High School girl, has given a vivid portrait of growing up in the middle-class suburbs close to Queen Alexandra Road during the 1950s in her autobiography *The Kindness of Strangers*:

> We lived on the outskirts of Sunderland, all neat gardens and dog-walking, with so little traffic that playing in the street was natural, punctuated with only one or two cries per morning of "There's a car coming!" We children had no concept of any threat to our existence and were a resoundingly boring example of quite well-mannered obedience. We didn't care, for we knew no different. There was a hint of another sort of life on the huge council estates

and in the alleys of the town's east end, but I'm ashamed to say that I was devoid of curiosity and felt that there was nothing wrong with complacency.

It was certainly true that the middle and working-class areas of Sunderland were distinct and that they could easily be distinguished by looking at the vast difference in statistics such as premature deaths and poverty. The middle classes avoided areas such as the East End, but as the council estates began to surround them it became less possible to avoid noticing signs of poverty. The inhabitants of High Barnes could not avoid commenting on the 'raggy lads', whose families had moved from the East End and Deptford to the Plains Farm council houses, coming down to Barnes School with holes in the seats of their trousers.

Bede Collegiate Schools in Durham Road opened in 1929 when Sunderland's higher grade schools moved from their West Park building. The Girls' (foreground) and Boys' (background) were separate establishments. They both had a high academic reputation. As for many of the town's public buildings in the first half of the 20th century, W. & T.R. Milburn were the architects.

Sunderland had areas of contrasting prosperity, but it is arguable that there were less social tensions than in Newcastle and the North Tyneside boroughs. This is possibly because some of the middle classes had a strong Nonconformist influence, like some of the working classes, or came from the Jewish community with similar values.

One common bond between all Wearsiders was a pride in Sunderland and its major achievements. World War Two had reversed the unemployment of the 1930s and the decline in shipbuilding in the 1930s. When the 600th anniversary of the first record of the first shipyard in what became 'the largest shipbuilding town in the world' was celebrated in 1946

J. Ramsay Gebbie, the chairman of the Wear Shipbuilders' Association, could confidently write: 'The craftsmen of Sunderland are without superior anywhere, and I look forward to a prosperous future for the Industry and its workpeople.'

The tanker *British Princess* going down the slipway at Laing's Deptford yard after being launched by Princess Elizabeth on 30 April 1946. This royal launch was very welcome in the year that the Wear celebrated 600 years of shipbuilding.

CHAPTER 2

An Expanding Town
1945–66

From War to Peace

At 4pm on Wednesday 8 May 1945, an hour after the broadcast of the Prime Minister, Winston Churchill, the Mayor of Sunderland, Councillor John Young, announced the surrender of the Germans. The area around the Town Hall was packed with an estimated 10,000 Wearsiders rejoicing at the end of the war in Europe. The celebrations continued with dancing on the terrace of Mowbray Park.

Part of the estimated crowd of 10,000 Wearsiders wait in Fawcett Street on 8 May 1945 to hear the Mayor announce the end of the war in Europe.

For some families on Wearside, however, there was limited rejoicing while their servicemen continued fighting the war in the Far East or still languished in Japanese prisoner of war camps. Their ordeal came to an end on 15 August 1945 when the surrender of Japan was announced and on 14 October the first batch of Far East prisoners of war returned home to a civic welcome.

The returning servicemen and women found a town in which German bombing had left noticeable gaps in the town centre. It was also a town in which war had produced full employment after the Depression of the 1930s and in which women were a significant part of the labour force and were even working in the shipyards. The women were, however, quickly made redundant from many jobs as men returned from the forces. In November 1945, for instance, the *Sunderland Echo* commented on the increased number of tram and bus conductors as they replaced conductresses after their return from war service.

The Mayor, John Young, welcoming home former Japanese prisoners of war, on 14 October 1945. They included members of the 125 Anti-Tank Regiment which had originally been a Territorial unit based in Sunderland. The regiment's soldiers had been captured at the fall of Singapore and experienced terrible suffering in POW camps.

Between the victories in Europe and Far East the first General Election since 1935 took place on 5 July 1945. As well as the two sitting 'National' (Conservative and National Liberal) MPs, two Labour candidates and a Communist candidate also stood in Sunderland.

On 29 June the *Echo's* reports on the election campaign contained an unusual apology. An 'unauthorised person' had inserted Communist leaflets into the previous night's paper. It seems very unlikely that any reader would have had any illusions about the *Echo* supporting any other than the National candidates, one of whom was the paper's proprietor, Samuel Storey. The front page stories always reported the National candidates' successful meetings and on polling day it urged readers to 'Vote Early and Vote National'. The following day the headline was 'Ballot Expected To Favour National Candidates'.

There was a three-week delay before the election results were announced to allow the votes of service personnel to be counted. When the declaration was announced on 26 July the result in Sunderland, as in the rest of the country, was a massive swing to Labour. Fred Willey and Richard Ewart replaced Samuel Storey and Stephen Furness as MPs.

Municipal elections followed on 1 November 1945. The contest was between Labour and the ruling Moderate party. The Moderates were in many ways the Conservatives under a different name, as until the late 1940s Conservatives argued that national politics should not be involved with local government.

The *Echo* inevitably backed the Moderates, but after the election they only had 29 Councillors as opposed to Labour's 43. The ballot by Councillors for an Alderman for each Ward added a further nine to Labour's majority. The selection of Aldermen by the Council rather than at the Council elections was a feature of municipal life until 1974. Inevitably they were members of the ruling party.

As in the national parliamentary elections, Labour's victory in the municipal elections produced some notable casualties. Sir Myers Wayman, Mayor for most of the war, was defeated in Humbledon Ward.

Labour in Power

The Labour Party's control of the Council in 1945 was to last for over 20 years, a period which was to see great changes in the town. In 1945 the new Council was faced with several challenges. The wartime bombing had destroyed both commercial and residential properties. In addition to their replacement a start had to be made on the slum clearance programme suspended in 1939. Building materials continued to be in short supply, a reflection of limited availability of many items during this period of austerity, which saw rationing continuing into the early 1950s.

The Labour government's extension of state control saw some reduction of the powers of the council. The municipal hospitals passed to the new National Health Service, although new responsibilities for residential care and for children were placed with the local authority.

The municipal electricity undertaking was nationalised along with the coal mines, gas, railway and road haulage services. The United buses also came under state control, unlike the Northern buses and Corporation buses and trams. A scheme to nationalise all passenger road transport in the North-East was in fact put forward in 1949, but was not pursued after the return of the Conservative government in 1951. The Conservatives soon returned most road haulage to the private sector.

Although it lost some powers in the late 1940s, the council gained other responsibilities, such as residential accommodation for the elderly and increased planning powers which led to the setting up of a separate planning department in 1962. Other departments covered a wide range of duties including roads, museums and libraries, parks and cemeteries, cleansing, seaside development, police and fire brigade. The work of the

George McIntire, Sunderland's Town Clerk from 1932 to 1962, in his Town Hall office. McIntire was in charge of Sunderland's administration during difficult periods including the Depression and the war when he was Civil Defence Controller. He was the father of Jane Grigson, the cookery writer.

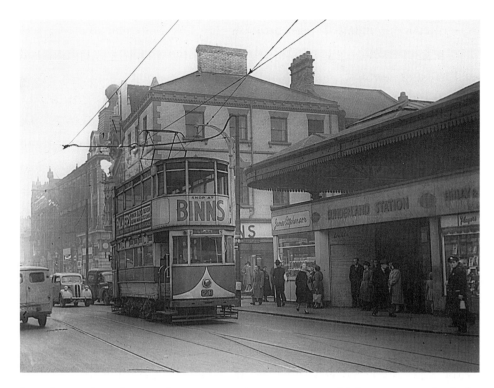

Tram 73 stands at the north end of Sunderland Central Station shortly after the railways were nationalised in 1948. The London and North Eastern Railway's logos have already been removed from either side of the Sunderland Station name.

housing, education and transport departments, which were particularly significant during this period, are discussed below.

One significant department was Public Health. It was this department that recommended which slum houses should be demolished as well as aiming to improve the relatively poor health of many Sunderland people in several other ways. In 1966 its services included health clinics, a home for unmarried mothers, home nursing services and the disinfection of premises, bedding and clothing.

The chairman of the Public Health Committee was Sir Jack Cohen, the Labour leader for most of the 1950s and 1960s; he was also chairman of the Sunderland Area Hospital Management Committee. Cohen was responsible for the building of a much-needed municipal abattoir in Fulwell in 1962 replacing 15 slaughterhouses, five of which were used by the wholesale trade. The Medical Officer of Health's reports in the 1940s and 1950s constantly stated that it was impossible to maintain a good standard of hygiene in the smaller of the town's slaughterhouses. They were totally inadequate and meat and offal

The Queen Mother opening the extended Central Library and Museum on 24 June 1964.

was often contaminated. The proposal for the municipal abattoir was bitterly opposed by the butchers who operated the smaller slaughterhouses on their own premises and during the controversy a pig's head was nailed to Cohen's back gate.

The new abattoir was one of several developments undertaken by the Council in the late 1950s and the 1960s as the financial restrictions of the years of austerity eased. The purchase of the Empire Theatre in 1959 to become the first theatre in the country to be acquired by a council was a significant development. The major extension to the Central Library and Museum in 1964 was a project which had been delayed from the 1930s and was accompanied by a programme of building new branch libraries.

The Conservatives were in power nationally for 13 years from 1951, and indeed also held the Sunderland South parliamentary seat from 1952 to 1964, but the Labour party continued to control the Council throughout this period. The stability of the political situation is shown by the fact that in the 1957 municipal elections in Sunderland only four out of 18 wards were contested. The turnout in these was 39.7 percent, showing that claims of voter apathy 40 years later were not a new phenomenon.

The Housing Estates

The greatest change to Sunderland in the 20 years after the end of World War Two was the growth of the large council housing estates encircling the built-up area of the 1930s. They were constructed to meet an acute shortage of homes in the immediate post-war period and, later, to house people moved from the substandard properties of the inner areas.

The building of housing was the Council's main post-war priority. One of the new Labour Council's first moves was to set up a Housing Committee; housing had previously been dealt with by the Health Committee.

Many of Sunderland's 19th-century houses were in a bad state and were overcrowded, particularly in the East End, Monkwearmouth, Deptford and parts of Hendon and Millfield. A survey in 1936 had shown that more than 20 percent of families lived in overcrowded properties compared with 3.8 percent nationally. Sunderland was the most overcrowded county borough in England and Wales.

The condition of the houses also placed Sunderland at the bottom end of comparative studies. The 1951 census recorded that 43 percent of Sunderland households either shared or were entirely without piped water, while 52 percent had no fixed bath. Many Sunderland families of four or five lived in two rooms of a house with the other two rooms upstairs being occupied by another family. Both families had to share a tap in the yard and the outside 'netty'.

Sunderland's poor standard of housing was in spite of the fact that nearly 5,000 houses had been built by the Council and 2,000 by the Special Housing Association before the outbreak of World War Two. War stopped the Council's programme of demolition for 1,918 dwellings and further increased the problem, as 1,200 houses were lost due to bombing, with an additional 35,000 suffering war damage.

The government's priority in the 1940s was to build new houses for families without a home of their own. Slum clearance was to be put on hold until 1953 when the government indicated that local authorities should resume their clearance programmes. Sunderland benefited from the policy of the new Conservative Minister of Housing, Harold Macmillan who in 1951 announced the government's intention to build 300,000 houses a year nationally (in both the public and private sectors).

While the poor quality of housing was the driving factor in moving families from the inner areas of Sunderland from the 1950s, there were other reasons for clearing these areas. Some suffered from environmental pollution produced by adjacent heavy industry. The clearance of houses also provided room for these industries, still the major employers in the town, to expand, as, for instance, Doxford's did at Low Pallion.

The need to build houses as soon as possible had been accepted by the Council in May 1945 when it was still under Moderate control. By August 1945 the first council 'temporary' house had been completed in Hendon.

A house in Coronation Street decorated to mark the Coronation of the Queen on 2 June 1953. Behind the exuberance of the decorations was a house which, like many other in the East End, was probably substandard.

Many of these prefabs were to be built in Sunderland during the next few years.

The majority of the new houses were in the estates of Penny-well, Grindon, Spring-well, Thorney Close, Farringdon, Carley

These prefabs in Hunter's Hall Road were among many hundreds built to meet the post-war housing shortage. They were modernised shortly after this photograph was taken in 1970 and survived into the 21st century.

A tram on the reserved track of the extension of the Durham Road tram route, opened in 1948 to Grindon Lane and in 1949 to Thorney Close Road to serve new housing. To the left is the 1930s Plains Farm Estate and to the right the recently-built Springwell Estate. The tram track was removed in 1954.

Looking over the Hetton Colliery Railway at North Moor in about 1949 to new council housing at Farringdon. Beyond Durham Road, which cuts across the middle of the photograph, are further houses under construction at Thorney Close. The darker houses to the right of the photograph are those of the pre-war Plains Farm Estate.

Hill, Witherwack, Hylton Red House, Hylton Castle and Town End Farm. All were all built on farmland beyond the pre-war suburbs. A boundary extension in the Pennywell, Farringdon and Red House areas was sanctioned in 1951 for new estates, but by 1966 housing extended to the edge of the extended municipal boundaries.

Nearly all the council properties in the 1950s were semi-detached houses with their own gardens and the estates were planned with open spaces at regular intervals. While shops and new schools were built to serve the new communities, those who moved from the inner areas of the towns complained about the lack of other amenities as well as the cost of travel. In their old homes most had walked to and from work, but now had to pay fares on trams and buses to reach their new houses. Many found the estates

with their open spaces a contrast with their former neighbourhoods. Town End Farm was nicknamed 'The Ponderosa' after the vast ranch of the television series of the 1950s and 1960s.

In the 1960s the Council began to construct two, three or four-storey maisonettes and a few tower blocks, particularly in the inner areas which had been cleared of their slum housing. The first multi-storey flats were completed in 1964.

St Anne's Roman Catholic Church in Pennywell. Replacing an earlier wooden building in South Hylton, it was built in 1957 to serve the new housing estate at Pennywell. Next to it is a Catholic primary school.

The record of Sunderland in building new municipal houses was outstanding. Aneurin Bevan, Minister of Health, who was responsible for housing, opened the 3,000th council property in 1949, Fred Willey MP the 15,000th in 1960 and Gordon Bagier MP the 20,000th, enough to rehouse a third of the population, in 1965. This was a higher total than had been achieved by any other County Borough in England or Wales. Although it had the best record for the number of houses built Sunderland was second bottom of the table for the size of dwellings; 59 percent had only one or two bedrooms.

The majority of housing development in Sunderland was by the council rather than private developers. Between 1940 and 1953 building licences were needed to construct new houses and Sunderland Council felt that the priority had to be their own programme and not private developments. New private housing was built during the 1950s and 1960s, notably at Seaburn Dene and south of Queen Alexandra Road, but in 1965 only 4,000 private houses had been built compared to the Council's 20,000. There was certainly a lack of private housing in the town and this led to some newly-married couples living outside the town, thus reducing its middle-class population.

The 15,000th council house at Brentford Square, Town End Farm Estate, which was opened by Fred Willey on 26 September 1960. The house had been furnished in contemporary style and was open to the public. It was described by the *Echo* as 'a "dream house" for the 1960s housewife designed to eliminate extra work'.

Education

Education was probably second to housing in the scale of the Council's priorities. By the mid 1960s the Local Education Authority remit included five colleges of further education, 34 secondary schools, 71 primary schools, five special schools and four nursery schools. All came under the Director of Education.

Monkwearmouth in 1963 with one of Sunderland's first tower blocks under construction on the site of demolished houses. On the right is Dock Street Methodist Church.

Sunderland Technical College had been founded in 1901 for apprentice students and had been the first education establishment to establish 'sandwich' courses. In the post-war years it was particularly noted for its pharmacy and naval architecture departments; the latter attracted students from Norway and other overseas centres. In the late 1950s it was decided to concentrate on seeking College of Advanced Technology status and a major expansion programme took place, culminating in the opening of the new Chester Road campus in 1964. By 1966 the Technical College had over 1,000 students from throughout Great Britain and from 26 overseas countries.

The other two Sunderland higher education establishments were both in Ashbrooke. The College of Art in Ashburne House, the former home of the Backhouse family, grew under the principalships of Richard Ray and Walter Norman and by 1960 had more than 1,000 students. The Training College for teachers, later the College of Education, in Langham Tower had been women-only until 1959. Its numbers grew from 250 to 600 in 1966 and eventually 800. It trained students for teaching in infant, junior and secondary schools.

When the Technical College concentrated on higher education its vocational courses were handed over to two new establishments. The Monkwearmouth College of Further Education provided vocational courses in business studies, dressmaking and nursing. West Park College of Further Education, on the other hand, concentrated on more 'male' apprentice craft training.

At the top of the state school system in Sunderland was 'The Bede', the Bede Boys' and Girls' Collegiate Schools, which had an excellent academic reputation, particularly for sending their pupils to Oxford, Cambridge and other universities. They were grammar schools which selected children by the 11-plus examination. The other grammar schools in the town were Monkwearmouth, which drew its pupils from the north side of the river, and St Aidan's and St Anthony's Roman Catholic Schools which catered for boys and girls respectively. Just outside the municipal boundary was Ryhope Grammar School, run by Durham County Council until 1967.

For those who had closely missed being selected for grammar school the West Park Central School was the next choice; it later became a girls-only school with an emphasis on commercial subjects. The Junior Technical School in Villiers Street produced a number of notable shipbuilders and engineers; in 1959 it moved to Ryhope Road to become Southmoor School.

The majority of children in Sunderland went on to secondary modern schools. These were often in the same buildings as the primary schools, but from the 1950s new secondary moderns were built in the new estates, such

The Duke of Edinburgh after opening Sunderland Technical College's new buildings in Chester Road. To the right of the Duke is the Mayor, Mrs Jane Hedley.

James Williams Street School was the first building erected by the Sunderland School Board in 1874. The 18 Board schools built in the years up to 1903 survived into the 1960s when they began to be replaced by new buildings.

The library at Monkwearmouth School, a new comprehensive in Seaburn Dene which replaced Monkwearmouth Grammar School in Swan Street. The former Grammar School became Monkwearmouth College of Further Education.

as Thorney Close, Farringdon and Broadway. Several new primary schools, 12 between 1947 and 1953, were built to serve the new housing, but most were housed in the Victorian and Edwardian buildings erected by the Sunderland School Board.

The most significant development in school education was the decision to introduce a comprehensive system whereby the 11-plus exam was abolished and all children would undertake their secondary education in neighbourhood schools. This was to be achieved by purpose-built comprehensives at Red House and Thornhill, Pennywell and Southmoor and converting the secondary moderns at Castle View, Broadway, Thorney Close and Farringdon and the Bede and Monkwearmouth Grammar Schools.

The Roman Catholic schools were dealt with separately as they were run in conjunction with the Church. The Catholic secondary modern of St Thomas Aquinas and the grammar schools of St Aidan and St Anthony all also became comprehensives, but the latter two retained their single sex status.

Red House, the first purpose-built comprehensive, opened in 1963 and the system was introduced in other areas during the mid-1960s. It proved extremely controversial when it was decided to end Bede's selective status. The arguments for the new system advanced by Ernest Armstrong, chairman of the education committee in the early 1960s, were based on increasing opportunity for all. He argued that selection at 11 closed too many doors for the majority of children at too early an age and that too many resources were concentrated on a relatively few star pupils at Bede. Those who opposed the changes argued that Bede had provided an opportunity for advancement to all Sunderland children, including those from working-class families who were now less likely to benefit from going to all-ability neighbourhood schools. They also stressed that, above all, a centre of academic excellence was being abolished. Inevitably the views of the Council, which reflected those of national government, prevailed and Bede became a comprehensive.

Private education was represented in the town by Sunderland High School for Girls (renamed the Church High School in 1957), administered by the local committee of the Church Schools Company, Tonstall Preparatory School and Argyle House, both of which were boys' schools. The High School expanded in the 20 years after the war both at its main building in Mowbray Road and at Hendon Hill, which it acquired for its preparatory department in 1946.

The Shopping Centres

In contrast to the expanding estates on the outskirts the town centre remained little changed until the mid 1960s with several of the bombed sites being filled only on a temporary basis. The biggest development was the rebuilding of Binns store, first on the west side of Fawcett Street in 1952 and then 10 years later by the east side building, which was linked by a subway under the street. Binns lost its independence when it was acquired by the Glasgow-based House of Fraser in 1953. Several of its departments, such as the garages and the painting and cabinetmaking sections, were subsequently closed down.

Binns's main rival, Joplings, also opened a new shop in John Street after fire destroyed its High Street premises in 1954. There were other smaller department stores including Blacketts, Liverpool House, Kennedys Cobden Exchange and Palmers. The national chains of Marks & Spencer, established in Sunderland since 1895, British Home Stores and Little-woods, who built their new store in 1966 on the site of the north entrance to the station, provided increased competition for the local firms as consumer spending increased from the 1950s.

The three national chain stores all had their branches in High Street

Fawcett Street in 1954 when Binns west store had been rebuilt, although it was a further eight years before a new store was rebuilt on the opposite side of the street. On the extreme left is the Northern Gas Office building which was eventually acquired by Binns.

Jopling's store after destruction by the fire of 14 December 1954, one of Sunderland's worst fires. Joplings had started in High Street East in the 1820s as Jopling and Tuer and moved to this site in 1919.

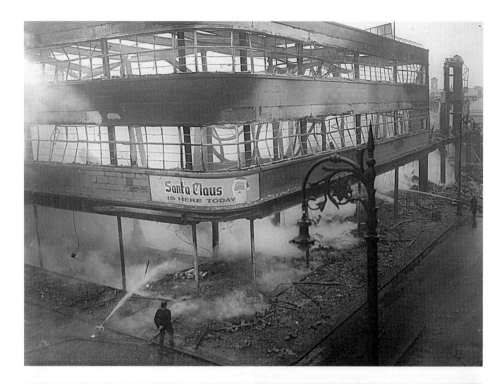

Joplings John Street store in the 1960s. It was opened in 1956, on the site of the bombed St Thomas Church, to replace the shop burnt down in 1954. The shop had Sunderland's first escalator – an attraction for many local children!

West, between Fawcett Street and Crowtree Road. This was also where the Sunderland Co-op opened their new main store after moving from Green Street. North of Binns, Fawcett Street housed the branches of Boots and Woolworths as well as several local shops, including Shares who sold furniture.

The local shopping centres in Hendon, Grangetown, Chester Road, Hylton Road, Pallion, Southwick and Fulwell and on the new estates still thrived throughout the 1950s and 1960s, but by the middle of the latter

High Street West looking west from Fawcett Street. This area had branches of several national chains. The single-storey building is British Home Stores while Marks and Spencer lies further west. The tall structure in the background is the Queen Street mill of E.C. Robson, who also operated Bishopwearmouth flour mill.

The Pennywell shopping centre in Portsmouth Road showing the wide range of shops from national chains such as Liptons and Woolworths to the Sunderland Co-op.

decade Monkwearmouth was starting to decline as the surrounding area was redeveloped and changes were made to the road system.

In addition to shops operated by their owners the local shopping centres would also have branches of local companies, such as the Co-op, Milburns

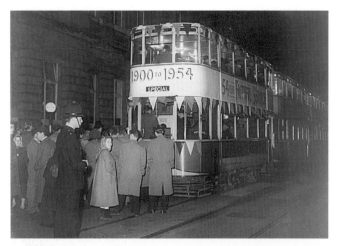

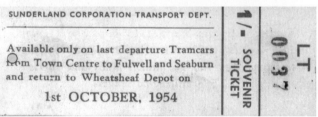

Sunderland's last tram, 86, prepares to leave the Town Hall as part of the final procession to Seaburn and then into the Wheatsheaf depot on 1 October 1954 and the souvenir ticket issued for those travelling in the final procession of tramcars.

The temporary Corporation bus station in Union Street which only lasted for five years from 1951. The bus on the left is in the old red and cream livery while that on the right is in the green and cream livery adopted in 1953. The 'Shop at Binns' advertisement was carried on Sunderland's municipal trams and buses for 50 years from the 1920s.

the Bakers and Chalks the Fruiterers as well as possibly of national chains such as Fine Fare which had taken over local retailers. The banks, such as Lloyds and Barclays, had branches in most of the local shopping centres as well as their town centre offices. Areas such as Pallion and Fulwell also still had their own cinemas, although the growth of television meant that the smaller picture houses were beginning to close.

The local shopping centres were still thriving and this was even more the case in the colliery villages where the Co-op was the major store. In Ryhope, for instance, the Ryhope and Silksworth Co-op had a large store with several departments, whose customers received a dividend payment on goods bought there. Even in the middle-class suburbs many women would still shop locally for items such as food, only going into town for clothes and specialist items or possibly to meet their friends for coffee, perhaps at the exclusive Mengs in the immediate post-war years or at Binns, Milburns or Lockharts.

Public Transport

In the 1940s and 1950s the expansion of the town meant that public transport became more significant as it was used by an increasing number of people to travel to work or to shop in the town centre. Local transport

was mainly provided by the Corporation or by the various bus companies. The London & North Eastern Railway (LNER), and then from 1948, British Railways, ran trains outside the County Borough boundaries to Newcastle, Durham, Middlesbrough and South Shields and other local towns as well as long-distance services.

Until the late 1950s ferries provided an older means of transport. The steam powered Sunderland ferry boats, operated by the Corporation between Monkwearmouth and the East End, ceased operation in 1957 following demolition of housing near the river. Outside the County Borough boundaries, the rowing boat ferry between South and North Hylton ceased in 1957 and that at Cox Green was replaced by a footbridge in 1958.

Sunderland Corporation had an extensive tramway system with several modern vehicles, but in 1947 it was decided to gradually replace trams by buses (which the Corporation had also operated since 1929). This was because of the expense of renewing track and overhead wires and the fact that new housing estates were being constructed away from the tram routes. There were, however, problems about obtaining new buses and it was agreed that the Durham Road tram route should still be extended to Thorney Close which was reached in 1949. In 1952 it was decided that the replacement programme should be speeded up and the last tram ran in October 1954.

New bus services were introduced to the growing housing estates on the outskirts of the town. Several of these were outside the Corporation's traditional operating area and were operated jointly with the Northern General Company and its Sunderland District subsidiary. These two companies worked most of the bus services to the north and west of Sunderland while the United Automobile Company and its Durham District subsidiary also operated services to the south. A major Corporation transport development in 1966 was the introduction of a flat fare system which was linked to the decision to convert the bus operations to one man single deckers.

Sunderland's passenger railway services radiated from the Central Station. This was a gloomy building situated in a cutting and whose roof had been damaged by wartime bombing. Sunderland Corporation pressed the LNER for a station more worthy of the town, but nothing, however, came of this. In 1966 the main entrance was moved to the south end. The north entrance was demolished and replaced by Littlewoods store, which with other shops above part of the station made it

The ferry across the Wear at Cox Green shortly before it was replaced by a footbridge in 1958. It was used by people travelling from some areas of Washington who caught the train from Cox Green station to Sunderland.

Barbara Castle, Minister of Transport, officially inaugurating the new flat fare system on Sunderland Corporation buses on 6 January 1967. She purchased a ticket by putting a token in the Autoslot machine below her left hand.

A new Corporation Leyland Panther bus on show in 1966 to advertise the flat fare system and tokens. Passengers purchasing tokens in advance at a discount on the normal fare would use the right-hand section of the entry door. The central door was for exit only.

The north end of Sunderland Central Station in 1964 looking towards High Street West. This was the main entrance which many Sunderland people recall as 'always smelling of fish'.

4-6-2 60146 *Peregrine* at Sunderland Central (undergoing rebuilding) with a Saturdays Only train from Newcastle to Butlin's Filey Holiday Camp on 8 August 1964, a reminder of how some Wearsiders spent their holidays before foreign package tours. A diesel multiple unit for Newcastle is on the left. The North end, whose tower, can be seen in the background was later demolished to make way for Littlewoods' store.

even more of a gloomy space. A number of train services using the station were withdrawn and by 1966 only the services to Newcastle and Middlesbrough remained.

Shipbuilding

In the 20 years after the end of World War Two, Sunderland's economy was still largely based on heavy industries such as shipbuilding, marine engineering and coal mining. In the 1950s almost a quarter of all men of working age were employed in shipbuilding and related industries.

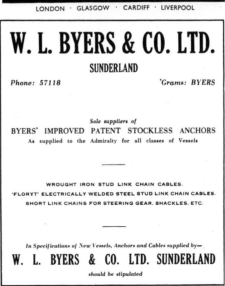

These advertisements of 1950 are a reminder that in addition to the workers employed in the yards shipbuilding was responsible for many jobs in firms supplying fittings to the industry. Speedings, almost alone among the companies supplying shipbuilding industries, has survived by diversifying into fire safety equipment and flags and banners.

The Wear yards continued to receive a steady supply of orders with vessels totalling an average of 218,000 tons being launched from the river between 1947 and 1956. The peak post-war year was 1958 when the tonnage was 268,000, although this was still below the peak year of 364,951 of 1906. The main problems in the immediate post-war years were not in fact orders, but the shortage of materials such as steel and to some extent the lack of skilled labour.

The figures for the tonnage of ships from the Wear masked the fact that fewer, but larger vessels were being built. The greatest demand was for bulk tankers which required bigger slipways than several yards had. Crown's overcame this in 1951 by building the 23,000 ton oil tanker *Rondefjell* in two parts before they were joined together in a dry dock on the Tyne. This could only be a short-term solution and the Crown's yard was soon absorbed into the larger North Sands operation of J.L. Thompson, who already owned Crown's. Short's yard at Pallion closed in 1964 because it lacked the capital to enlarge its berths for the bigger general cargo vessels which were now in demand.

The *Borgsten* leaving Thompson's North Sands yard in 1963. This 65,000 ton vessel was the largest British built tanker and the biggest merchant ship built in the country for many years.

Several of the other Wearside yards enlarged their berths to build the bigger ships. The need to have a wider financial base to do this and also to share technical facilities led to mergers of the different companies. In 1954 Austin's and Pickersgill's yards merged with a major £3 million redevelopment of the Pickersgill's yard taking place. After 1957 the capital for the scheme came from London and Overseas Freighters which took over the company. Further development took place in the 1960s and the company also pioneered several technological advances. Austin's yard closed in 1964.

There had long been managerial links between Laing's and J.L. Thompson's yards and the Sunderland Forge. In 1954 the Sunderland Shipbuilding, Dry Dock and Engineering Company was set up to incorporate these as well as Greenwell's ship repairing yard, Wolsingham Forge and Lynn's who manufactured winches. A further merger with Doxford's shipyard and engineering works in 1961 created the Doxford and Sunderland Shipbuilding and Engineering Company. Bartram's worked increasingly closely with Austin and Pickersgill.

Both Laing's and Thompson's modernised their yards. Laing's built a large berth on the site of the Deptford Bottleworks and two old berths were consolidated into one. Thompson's modernisation was even more extensive, taking in the surrounding streets as well as Crown's old yard. The 65,000 ton *Borgsten* was the largest British tanker ever built when it was launched in 1963.

Twenty years after the end of war the optimism of the 1940s had evaporated and doubts were increasing about whether even all the modernised yards on the Wear could survive. Laing's future had been under threat in 1960, but it was rescued by orders for two 19,000 tankers for BP. In 1966 the Doxford and Sunderland group was envisaging a substantial loss and closure of the Pallion yard, which had produced most tonnage on the Wear every year bar one up to 1962. The closure did not, however, happen.

The uncertainty on the Wear in the mid-1960s reflected growing national concern about the increased competition from shipyards in countries such as Japan and the decline of the British ship owners who had traditionally placed orders with certain yards. On the Wear, for instance, Doxford's traditionally received orders from the Bank Line and J. Reardon Smith of Cardiff.

This national concern led to the *Report of the Shipbuilding Enquiry Committee* chaired by R.M. Geddes. In 1966 this recommended that shipyards should merge into larger units and that there should be only one concern on the Wear. This was not to be accepted in Sunderland where Austin and Pickersgill, which would have been the junior partner in any proposed merger, was developing what was to prove a world-beating design. Instead Austin and Pickersgill took over Bartram's in 1968.

Marine engineering was of course closely linked to shipbuilding and Doxford's were involved in both. Doxford's had pioneered the development of the marine diesel engine as far back as 1912 and had achieved pre-eminence in the inter-war years. In the 1930s 90 percent of the world's diesel engines were built to Doxford's design. In addition to those built at Pallion 14 other firms built them, including companies in the US, Canada and Holland. Doxford's continued to develop their engines, including their first turbo-charged engine in the 1960s, but their share of the market dropped following competition from Sulzer and Burmeister. They nevertheless remained a major player in world marine engineering.

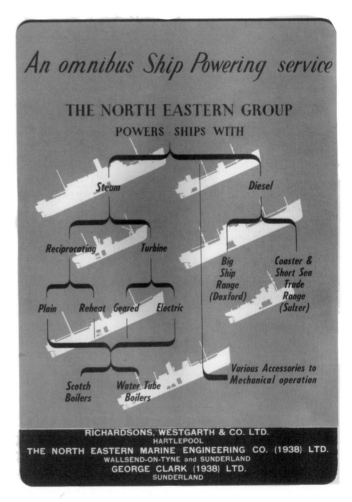

This 1950 advertisement for the North Eastern Group, which had two marine engine works in Sunderland, illustrated the wide range of power packages they provided for ships.

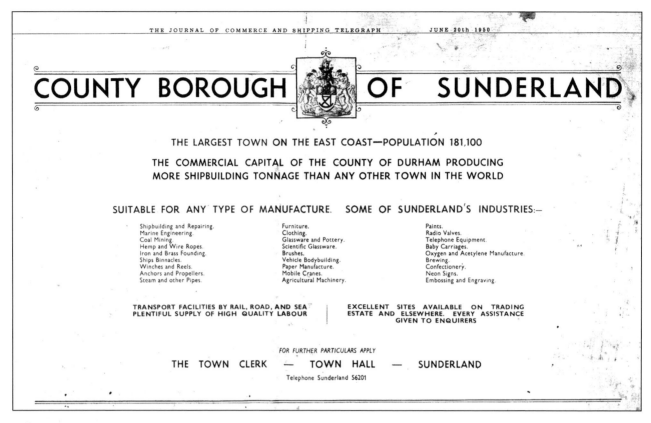

THE JOURNAL OF COMMERCE AND SHIPPING TELEGRAPH   JUNE 20th 1950

COUNTY BOROUGH OF SUNDERLAND

THE LARGEST TOWN ON THE EAST COAST—POPULATION 181,100

THE COMMERCIAL CAPITAL OF THE COUNTY OF DURHAM PRODUCING
MORE SHIPBUILDING TONNAGE THAN ANY OTHER TOWN IN THE WORLD

SUITABLE FOR ANY TYPE OF MANUFACTURE.   SOME OF SUNDERLAND'S INDUSTRIES:—

Shipbuilding and Repairing.	Furniture.	Paints.
Marine Engineering.	Clothing.	Radio Valves.
Coal Mining.	Glassware and Pottery.	Telephone Equipment.
Hemp and Wire Ropes.	Scientific Glassware.	Baby Carriages.
Iron and Brass Founding.	Brushes.	Oxygen and Acetylene Manufacture.
Ships Binnacles.	Vehicle Bodybuilding.	Brewing.
Winches and Reels.	Paper Manufacture.	Confectionery.
Anchors and Propellers.	Mobile Cranes.	Neon Signs.
Steam and other Pipes.	Agricultural Machinery.	Embossing and Engraving.

TRANSPORT FACILITIES BY RAIL, ROAD, AND SEA | EXCELLENT SITES AVAILABLE ON TRADING
PLENTIFUL SUPPLY OF HIGH QUALITY LABOUR | ESTATE AND ELSEWHERE. EVERY ASSISTANCE
GIVEN TO ENQUIRERS

FOR FURTHER PARTICULARS APPLY

THE TOWN CLERK — TOWN HALL — SUNDERLAND

Telephone Sunderland 56201

The advertisement by Sunderland Council in the *Journal of Commerce and Shipping Telegraph's* special issue to mark the centenary of South Docks in 1950. It shows the wide range of industries in the town in addition to shipbuilding.

The two other marine engineering works were North Eastern Marine (NEM) at the South Docks and George Clark at Southwick which in 1945 were still manufacturing steam marine engines. The two firms, which were part of the same group, merged in 1957 and the South Docks works closed in 1962. By 1952 George Clark had switched to manufacturing diesel engines built to Sulzer designs.

In addition to the shipyards and marine engine works there were many other concerns supplying material for shipbuilding. These included the several forges in the town which, of course, made castings for other customers.

Industry

In addition to shipbuilding the mining and transport and shipping of coal were of major importance to Sunderland. Coal was also vital for the nation's economy and the National Coal Board undertook substantial investment. It was clear that the future of mining in County Durham lay in the coastal pits. In the 1950s a start was made on modernising Wearmouth Colliery along with the other 'super pits' near the sea.

As well as investing in the larger pits, the NCB was also closing smaller mines and in 1966 production ceased at Ryhope. Some miners moved to Wearmouth, which looked as if it had a bright future; drilling off the

Sunderland coast had established that there were 500 million tons of workable coal.

Coal was the most significant railway and sea traffic in Sunderland. The National Coal Board operated its own trains which ran to the staiths below the bridge (until 1967) as well as to the South Dock. Coal was also the most important traffic on the main line railways in the area. The hub of the British Railways coal operation was the yard at South Dock. Here the wagons were shunted onto the staiths and coal was dropped into the ships below, which were often bound for the gas and electricity works of south-east England.

During the 1950s some of Sunderland's traditional industries disappeared completely. The closure of the limestone quarry and works at Fulwell and the Wearside Pottery marked the end of industries which went back to the 18th century. Turnbull's, the last traditional pressed glass manufacturer, also went out of business, but James A. Jobling thrived. In addition to Pyrex, whose production increased by 94 percent between 1946 and 1958, they were manufacturing vast quantities of car headlamp lenses in the 1950s; four million were made in 1954. By 1960 the

In this view taken from Fencehouses station in 1959 the scene is dominated by the Lambton Coke Works. The headgear of Lambton D Colliery, closed in 1965, can just be made out behind the houses.

The harbour mouth and Docks area around 1970 looking from the south. Shipbuilding, ship repairing and marine engine works occupy much of the north bank of the Wear and the east side of the South Docks. On the west side of the Docks are the coal staiths and railway sidings.

South Docks showing the world's first aluminum bascule bridge which was opened by Alfred Barnes, Minister of Transport, in November 1946. In the background a locomotive is shunting coal wagons on the staiths.

manufacture of ordinary glass had become uneconomic and Jobling's concentrated on making heat resistant glass. There could have been few homes in Britain which did not have Pyrex table or cookware.

Several Sunderland firms such as Coles Cranes, part of the Steels Group, also expanded greatly during this period. Vaux Breweries grew not only by expanding its Sunderland site, but also by the acquisition of Usher's in Edinburgh and Ward's in Sheffield and by developing Swallow Hotels. The Cowie Group expanded from a single shop selling motorcycles in Millfield to a firm which had car dealerships across the north of England and the south of Scotland.

Other new firms were established on the industrial and trading estates at Pallion, Southwick, Hendon and Pennywell. The products included aero engine components, furniture, radio and television components, telephones and clothing. As in the case of mail order firms, several of the new businesses employed a largely female workforce, a major change to the normal employment pattern in the town.

2-8-0 90445 in the centre of the mass of railway sidings at the South Docks in 1965. On both sides of the locomotive are lines up to the staiths for shipping coal. In the right background are the tops of the electrically powered conveyor belts also used for loading coal.

A Bristol Britannia airliner flies over the Bristol Aero Engines factory in the Pallion Trading Estate where components for the plane's engines had been made. The company later became Rolls-Royce.

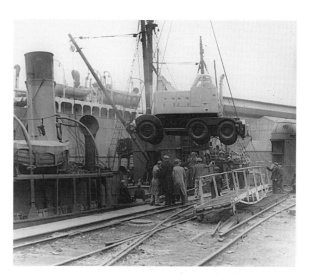

The body of one of Coles Cranes's mobile units being loaded at South Docks for export in the 1950s. These yellow cranes were a familiar sight in Britain and abroad for many years; a rail-mounted design was also produced.

An advertisement for Pyrex in 1954. The designs would have been familiar to most people living in Britain at the time.

Clerks checking orders at Brian Mills mail order depot in Hendon. This was an important source of mainly female employment from the 1950s and was a major business. In the late 1960s an average of four trains on weekdays left the depot's sidings with customers' orders.

Mixing bowls being packed for transport at the Wearside Pottery Works in Millfield; its products were exported as well as being sold in the home market. This was the last of Sunderland's potteries when it closed in 1957. In its latter years it had concentrated on yellow ware for kitchen use.

Edward Thompson workers checking sheets of bingo tickets in the 1960s. The headscarves hid the curlers the women were wearing; they would then comb their hair into fashionable bouffant styles to go out in the evening.

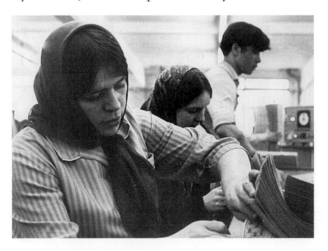

The *Sunderland Municipal Handbook* of 1966 recorded that the numbers of people in light industry and service employment had increased by over 11,000 in the previous 10 years. It nevertheless stated that: 'Whilst the number of men employed in Sunderland's traditional industries – such as shipbuilding, marine engineering and coal mining – is declining, the dominance of such industries is still apparent.'

CHAPTER 3

The Years of Change 1967–1991

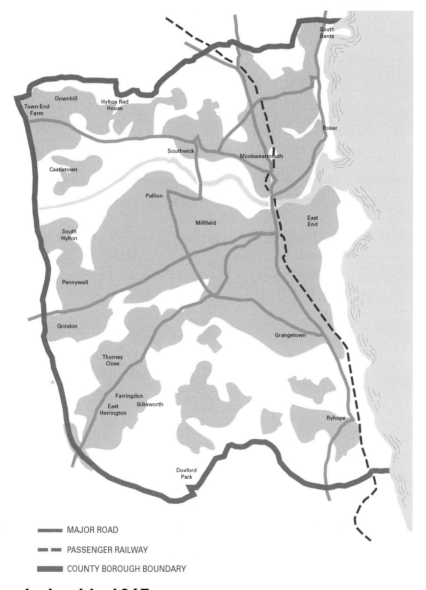

The County Borough of Sunderland in 1971.

▬▬▬ MAJOR ROAD

▬ ▬ PASSENGER RAILWAY

▰▰▰ COUNTY BOROUGH BOUNDARY

Sunderland in 1967

1967 was a year that saw several significant developments in Sunderland. The Labour group, which had controlled the Council since 1945, lost power to the Conservatives for five years. This was particularly galling for Labour as a number of the Council's long-term ambitions were achieved

The Miners' Hall in Silksworth shortly after the village became part of the enlarged County Borough. With the rundown of the pit the Miners' Hall, which was used by many organisations, closed in 1969. Like Ryhope and Castletown, Silksworth was a mining community.

during 1967. These included the incorporation of Sunderland Rural District, which included Ryhope, Silksworth, Castletown, East Herrington and South Hylton, into the County Borough of Sunderland along with the South Bents area of Whitburn.

A start was also made on the building of the new town centre and plans were well advanced for the new Civic Centre in West Park to replace the Town Hall. On the housing front proposals were being drawn up for a new

Looking from Stockton Road towards the newly-completed Civic Centre in 1970. On the left is West Park College of Further Education with West Park School (soon to be demolished) beyond.

'Silksworth Township' of 20,000 people (later named Doxford Park). In education the comprehensive system was being introduced and the Technical College and College of Art were chosen to become one of the country's first 30 polytechnics.

Not all the developments of 1967 were welcomed in the town. The amalgamation of the Sunderland Borough Police with the Durham Constabulary was not a popular move. Indeed the van carrying the new Durham County paperwork was only allowed to enter the Borough boundaries after midnight on the day of the takeover.

During the next 30 years Sunderland Council was to become very used to sharing or ceding some of its powers to other local authorities, government quangos and ultimately the private sector. The Council's role also changed greatly with new municipal housebuilding coming to an end and emphasis being placed on economic development in the face of growing unemployment as Sunderland's heavy industries declined. In 1970, for instance, the Council built its first industrial unit, something that had previously been done only by government bodies.

The policies of the national governments during this period had a major impact on Sunderland. This was particularly the case after the return of the Conservative administration headed by Margaret Thatcher in 1979. In addition to being unsympathetic to local government, it was also unwilling to continue to assist traditional heavy industries, particularly if they were state controlled, considering it better to invest in new forms of employment.

Industry and Employment

The most important factor in the history of Sunderland in the quarter century from 1967 was the dramatic decline of the town's traditional industries, which proved terminal in several cases. In their place came several new sources of employment. Not only did this transform the economic base of the town, it also changed the physical appearance of Wearside. The centre of industry moved away from the river banks to a corridor close to the new A19 road.

34,000 jobs were lost in the 10 years from 1971, mainly in the traditional industries, but also, more worryingly, in some of the post-war firms. By January 1986 the unemployment figures for the town were 22.7 percent compared with 19.5 percent for the northern region and 13.9 percent for the whole country. As well as the national 'job creation' programmes, certain areas of Sunderland were designated to receive special economic help in view of their high unemployment.

Silksworth Colliery shortly before closure in 1971, in spite of being modernised by the National Coal Board a few years before.

Police protecting miners who had returned to work at Wearmouth Colliery during the 1984–5 strike.

The Lambton Staiths on 5 January 1967, the day after the last shipment of coal had taken place. The electricity works dominate the left background of this photograph.

The fate of shipbuilding, which is described later, dominated the headlines in Sunderland for much of this period. It was accompanied by the rundown of other traditional industries, notably the mining and transport of coal. Ryhope, Silksworth, Elemore, Eppleton, Washington F, Glebe, Usworth, Hylton, Herrington and Houghton collieries and Lambton Coke Works all closed in the 20 years from 1966, leaving only Wearmouth Colliery, where workings were extended further under the sea in this period, to survive into the 1990s.

The closure of the collieries had a severe impact on the pit villages where they had been the major employers. The villages tended to be close-knit communities and this was reflected in the solid support for the National

Union of Mineworkers as was shown, for instance, in the 1974 strike over pay which effectively brought down the Conservative Government. Some splits, however, did appear during the 12-month long strike of 1984–5 in opposition to pit closures and the campaign ended in defeat for the NUM.

The export of coal from Sunderland ceased during this period. The Lambton Staiths closed in 1967. The staiths at the South Docks remained as a major shipping point for coal being transported to electricity power stations in the south-east of England. In 1983 1,570,529 tons of coal were shipped from the Docks, although some coal was starting to go direct by rail to power stations in Yorkshire and at Blyth. The opening in 1985 of the new coal handling facilities at Tyne Dock with capacity to handle larger vessels led to the closure of the South Docks staiths and conveyor belts in 1986.

The Port of Sunderland suffered in other ways from the decline of Sunderland's traditional industries, whose raw material was imported through the docks, although the import and storage of oil remained a significant traffic. New traffic, such as the *Baco* vessels which served Nigeria, was obtained for a period. However, planned roll-on roll-off facilities were not completed at the North Dock and the limit on the size of vessels and the storage area available for cargo remained a bar to the development of the South Docks.

Losses to the town's economy included several of the local foundries. Some of the foundries relied partly on shipbuilding for their orders, but they also had other work. E. Jopling of Pallion, for instance, had patented a successful new method of producing chains, but was closed down immediately after it was taken over by a new owner in 1986.

Takeover of Sunderland firms by both national and multinational companies was a marked feature of Sunderland's industry at this period. There was always a danger that in the drive to increase profitability 'branch' factories would be closed, but there were also occasions when the efficiency of the Sunderland operation led to its expansion. After James A. Jobling was taken over by the Corning International Corporation in 1973 production both of Pyrex domestic ware and of industrial glass was expanded with new facilities being built. Modernisation of industrial processes often meant, however, less rather than more jobs.

The tug *Dunelm* loading barges for Nigeria into *Baco-Liner 2* at Corporation Quay in the early 1980s. This was an important new trade for the port until it stopped because of political instability in the west African country. New cranes were installed on Corporation Quay to load containers on to the decks of the Baco vessels.

File making at Cook and Nicholson. This Monkwearmouth firm was one of the last in the county to make files. Its market declined as the demand by industry for files fell greatly and instead of manufacturing it started to import files in the late 1980s. The business was taken over by the neighbouring brush manufacturing firm of Cottams who still sold a handful of files each month in the early 2000s.

Advertisement in 1975 for Corning, who had taken over Joblings two years earlier. The Sunderland firm had held the British manufacturing rights for Pyrex from Cornings since 1921. The advertisement shows the scientific and industrial ware as well as the domestic Pyrex made in Sunderland.

SUNDERLAND GLASS

Has been famous for 1300 years since the days of the Venerable Bede.

World Famous now as PYREX consumer, scientific and industrial glassware manufactured at Wear Glass Works since 1922 by. . .

CORNING LIMITED
FORMERLY JAMES A. JOBLING & CO. LTD.

Another firm to pass into American ownership was Coles Cranes, which after a period of ownership by Acrow, became part of Grove, which had a worldwide operation in 1984. Fears were expressed about the Sunderland plant, but they appeared to be quelled when it was expanded. Many Sunderland plants, such as Rolls-Royce Aero Engines, experienced mixed fortunes during this period with expansion and cutbacks taking place according to the state of the order books.

Some of the new industries that had been attracted to the town since the war either closed or were greatly reduced in size. This was the case in television components and in radio and electronic equipment and, to some extent, in the mail order firms based at Hendon.

Although there was much gloom about the state of employment and industry on Wearside the town was successful in attracting several new industries. Above all was the golden prize of Nissan's new European car plant. Nissan decided to establish a new manufacturing centre in Britain in 1981. The project was, however, delayed and it was not until 1984 that an agreement was reached with the British government that the plant should go ahead.

Sunderland offered the relatively little-used municipal airfield site and surrounding land at Washington for the new factory. A key factor in the Wearside bid was that all options on the land needed had been secured and, unlike competing sites, 8,000 acres were immediately available. Tyne and Wear County Council, the Borough Council and Washington Development Corporation worked extremely closely together and maximised the grants available to the firm. In March 1984 it was announced that the Washington bid had been successful and in June work started on the site and the first Bluebird car came off the production line in July 1986.

The success in attracting Nissan, the largest Japanese economic investment in Europe and the biggest industrial development in the North-East cannot be overestimated. It was excellent publicity for the area and it also led to other Far Eastern firms setting up in the region. Some were directly related to Nissan. Ikeda-Hoover, which manufactures car seats and interior trims, was only one of several component suppliers to be established in the area.

Shipbuilding

It was perhaps ironic that a Japanese firm should have been so significant in starting the economic regeneration of Wearside, as one reason for the decline of the shipyards was competition from Japan. Shipbuilding had always been an industry that was affected by peaks and troughs, but the situation of all British yards deteriorated as the number of ships built in the Far East, at lower costs than in Europe, increased. At the same time the British merchant marine's tonnage fell from 23 million in 1975 to 8.5 million in 1987 and many of the Wear yards' traditional customers went out of business. Sunderland's last shipowning company, the Rose Line, sold its final ship in 1968. There was also a massive collapse in ship orders from 1975 after the oil crisis.

1967 saw a notable development in shipbuilding on the Wear with the launch of the first SD14, a standard design general cargo vessel which was intended to replace the Liberty ships. The SD14s were designed at Austin and Pickersgill under the direction of its managing director, Ken Douglas. 211 were built in the next 20 years, not only at Austin and Pickersgill's and Bartram's yards, but elsewhere, some in countries as far afield as Argentina and Vietnam.

Austin and Pickersgill's Southwick shipyard underwent a £3.5 million modernisation

The clearance of the derelict shipyard sites was a feature of Wearside during the last 30 years of the 20th century. Austin's yard, below the Wearmouth Bridge, had closed in 1964, but it was not cleared until the early 1970s. In the 1990s student accommodation was built on the far side of the yard.

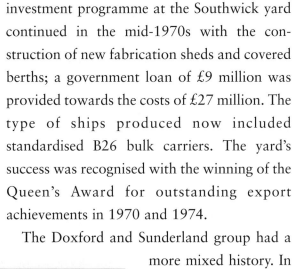

The *Naess Crusader* being completed at the North Sands yard in 1972. This was one of a number of huge 150,000-ton ore bulk tankers built at North Sands in the 1970s.

An SD14 cargo vessel being constructed by the night shift at Austin and Pickersgill's Southwick yard about 1980. The SD14 14,000-ton design was one of the outstanding merchant ship designs of its period.

The SD14 *Luc-Nam* about to be launched from one of the undercover bays at the Southwick yard on 12 December 1979. As its Vietnamese owners did not send anyone to launch the ship a draw was made from the names of A&P's female employees and the ceremony was performed by Iris Lindsay, a canteen assistant.

programme in the mid-1960s to allow the production of SD14s and other vessels. The investment programme at the Southwick yard continued in the mid-1970s with the construction of new fabrication sheds and covered berths; a government loan of £9 million was provided towards the costs of £27 million. The type of ships produced now included standardised B26 bulk carriers. The yard's success was recognised with the winning of the Queen's Award for outstanding export achievements in 1970 and 1974.

The Doxford and Sunderland group had a more mixed history. In 1972 Court Line, originally a shipping line, but now largely a travel business which already owned Appledore shipyard in Devon, took over the company. Jim Venus, the managing director of Appledore, was put in charge of the Sunderland operation and the remaining members of the shipbuilding families soon left the board of Sunderland Shipbuilders. One of the reasons for the takeover was that Court Line could provide the capital for investment in the Sunderland yards and this led to a start in 1973 on the construction of a completely covered yard at Doxford's in Pallion. This was the largest enclosed shipbuilding yard in the world with most of the processes being carried out under one roof.

Before the Pallion yard had been completed Court Line went into liquidation because of problems with its travel business. The new Labour government decided to nationalise Sunderland Shipbuilders to save the yards; there were no private bidders on the horizon in spite of healthy order books. Nationalisation of the other shipyards in Great Britain, including Austin and Pickersgill, followed in 1977 when British Shipbuilders were formed.

The two groups on the Wear continued at first to operate separately. The market for the large vessels, such as 150,000-ton bulk carriers, built at North Sands was, however, declining and the *Badagary Palm* was the last ship to be launched from the yard in 1979. Deptford, which had also been building bulk carriers, ceased production in 1985.

Austin and Pickersgill's Southwick Shipyard in 1982 showing the fabrication sheds and, in the distance, the covered berths constructed during the modernisation of the yard in 1975–7. On the south bank is A&P's second fitting out quay on the site of Short's Shipyard.

In addition to the shipyards, British Shipbuilders took over Doxford's Engine Works; Sunderland's other marine engine works, North Eastern Marine (incorporating George Clark), had already closed. During the 1970s Doxford's Seahorse engine had been a success, but in 1980 it was decided to close the works. The decision was, however, rescinded and a new £4.2 million crankshaft facility was opened in 1983. Following a change in the chairmanship of British Shipbuilders, however, Doxford's ceased production in 1984.

The modernised yards at Southwick and Pallion became part of North East Shipbuilders in 1986. In 1983 Austin and Pickersgill's order book of 30,000 and 36,000-ton bulk carriers had been the best in the United

Kingdom, but only a few years later it was running down towards closure. A lifeline was thrown to the Pallion yard when North East Shipbuilders obtained an order to build 24 ferries for Danish

Sunderland Shipbuilders' Manor Quay fitting out quay in 1983 with the *Marcos Lycas* and two other vessels. It seems hard to believe that, five years after this scene of shipbuilding activity, shipbuilding would come to an end on the Wear.

A Doxford J-type 8-cylinder
engine under construction at
Pallion Works. The first of this
type was built in 1964 and the
last in 1988.

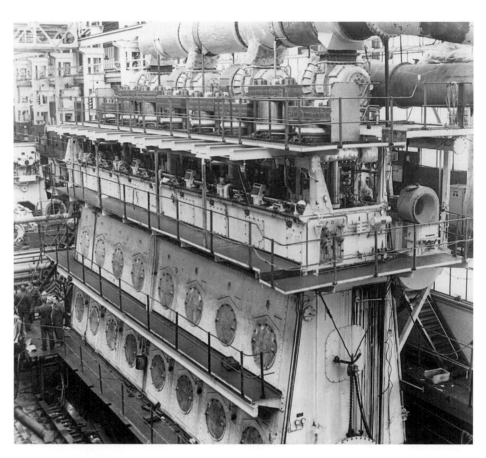

owners, but contractual difficulties over the vessels hastened the end of not
only the Pallion yard, but of all shipbuilding on the Wear, in 1988.

The future of Wear shipbuilding had already been thrown into doubt by
the decision of the re-elected Conservative government in 1987 to privatise
the yards owned by British Shipbuilders. The Govan yards on the Clyde
were sold off first with a grant for modernisation to the new owners. The

The Danish ferry *Superflex Kilo*
is floated out of the covered
shipbuilding hall at Pallion,
following its sister *Superflex
November* on 12 December
1988. This was one of the
saddest days in Sunderland's
history as the two ferries were
the last ships to be built on the
Wear.

European Economic Commission's agreement to this was to include a secret acceptance by Britain that meant that shipbuilding could not continue on the Wear. Tony Newton, the Minister of State at the Department of Trade and Industry, only became aware of this at a later date when he was still hoping to sell the Wear yards.

There had been a vigorous 'Save Our Shipyards' campaign in Sunderland to retain the industry for the town, but this came to nothing in the face of the Government/EEC agreement. Measures to aid the development of new jobs, including £45 million aid and the creation of two Enterprise zones, were announced in 1988, but a condition of this was that shipbuilding could not resume on the Wear for 10 years.

Even against the background of the fall in British-owned ships and the rise of shipbuilding in the Far East, the decline and ultimate end of shipbuilding on the Wear seemed hard to accept and was more significant than the loss of 2,000 jobs. The good record of the local yards and marine engine works and the tens of millions of pounds spent on upgrading them during the 1970s ultimately counted for nothing. The fact that Swan Hunter's yard on the Tyne survived because of the more secure naval orders and that closure of the Wear yards seemed partly the result of bureaucratic bungling made the end of shipbuilding more difficult to take.

The Last Years of the County Borough

The Conservative Group, which took power in 1967, broadly continued several of the policies of the previous administration in areas such as education and social services. A major objective of William Martin, the chairman of the Finance Committee, and the most powerful figure among the Conservatives, was to run the Council more efficiently and keep the rates down. The means of achieving this included reducing the number of council houses being built and abolishing the bus flat fare system; this led to the resignation of Norman Morton, the Corporation Transport General Manager. At the same time some new developments, including the Crowtree Leisure Centre, were planned.

The loss of power led to a major shakeup in the Labour Group. In 1968 Sir Jack Cohen resigned as leader when it was clear that he was about to be defeated in the Group election by Charles Slater, ironically his nephew. The 'old guard' Labour Aldermen lost their seats to the ruling Conservatives and control of the Labour Group passed to younger members under Slater's leadership.

Labour regained power in 1972, implementing its policy of immediately

Jim Gardner was Town Clerk of Sunderland between 1970 and 1973 and was involved with widening the role of the Council beyond providing municipal services to economic development. He left Sunderland to become Chief Executive of Tyne and Wear County Council and gained the nickname 'Tokyo Jim' for his travels to Japan to help secure the Nissan plant for Washington. After the County's abolition he served on several regional and national bodies.

increasing rates to improve services. Major changes to council powers were, however, already in view with the decision of the Conservative government to reform local government and establish a two-tier system throughout the country. This was to lead to the creation of Tyne and Wear County Council and an enlarged Borough of Sunderland.

1972 also saw the end of the River Wear Commissioners after 225 years when their powers and the Docks they ran passed to Sunderland Council. This was recognition of the Council's ultimate financial responsibility for the port, as it was the guarantor for the Commission's mortgages of almost £3 million without having complete control. In addition the different interests represented on the Commission's board, which included shipowners, shipbuilders, importers and exporters, meant it was difficult to secure agreement on where capital expenditure should be targeted.

The mid-1970s were a period when charges of corruption in local northeast government associated with the architect John Poulson led to the jailing of Andrew Cunningham and T. Dan Smith, the leading members of Durham County and Newcastle City Councils. The corruption charges did not touch Sunderland, apart from the fact that Cunningham, as chairman

Bobby Kerr, the Sunderland AFC Captain, holding the FA Cup aloft after the team beat Leeds in the Final at Wembley on 5 May 1973. Jimmy Montgomery, the goalkeeper, is sporting the lid of the cup on his head. To the right of Montgomery is Ian Porterfield, the scorer of the winning goal. For most Wearsiders this match, rather than any local government changes, was by far the most important event of the 1970s.

of the Durham Police Authority, had ensured that Poulson designed the new Sunderland Police Station.

In the mid-1960s T. Dan Smith had spoken to the Sunderland Labour Group about his vision for Newcastle as the new Brasilia of the north of England and offered the services of his consultancy to help Sunderland advance on the same lines. After he left the Group meeting Sir Jack Cohen had wisely said that they should have nothing more to do with Smith. Twenty years after the Poulson prosecutions allegations about corruption involving Sunderland councillors and council officers in the late 1980s were investigated by the police, but no charges were brought.

The County Council and the New Borough of Sunderland

The decision to establish Tyne and Wear County Council in 1974 meant that services that had previously been run by the County Borough were now divided between two local authorities. This would have been complex enough, but what made Sunderland people alarmed at the proposals was the decision to group Sunderland with Newcastle, Gateshead and the local authorities north and south of the Tyne into a new county called Tyneside! Following the intervention of Fred Willey MP, the name was changed to the more geographically accurate Tyne and Wear.

The creation of Tyne and Wear cut across Sunderland's traditional links with East Durham, for which the town was the commercial and shopping centre. This was accentuated by the drawing of the boundaries of the new Borough of Sunderland. As well as the County Borough, it included the Urban Districts of Hetton, Houghton and Washington (see map on page 136). The initial proposal to include Seaham in the Borough and Tyne and Wear was withdrawn. This was largely due to the lobbying of the Conservative government by local Conservatives who pointed out that leaving Seaham out would make Tyne and Wear more evenly balanced politically. The Conservatives later came within a few seats of controlling the County. On the other hand the addition of several former mining areas to the new Borough meant that a Labour majority on the Borough Council was even more secure.

Boldon Urban District, which included Cleadon and Whitburn, could also have been included in Sunderland Borough. It was, however, placed in South Tyneside Borough. This was the smallest Metropolitan Borough in the country, and it was doubtless felt essential to include Boldon in that district to ensure its viability.

There was no surprise at Hetton and Houghton being in Sunderland
Borough, but Washington could equally well have been part of Gateshead.
It was to be, however, a significant addition to the Borough because it had
been designated a New Town in 1964 to offset the decline of many of the
pit villages in North Durham. The Washington Development Corporation
was then established to plan the new town with an emphasis on providing
new employment and housing.

In 1974 those members who had moved from the County Borough to
the new Borough of Sunderland Council found themselves in charge of a
considerably larger geographical area, but one in which they shared
powers with the Tyne and Wear County Council and, in Washington, with
the Development Corporation.

The new Tyne and Wear County Council was generally unloved in
Sunderland. There was a strong dislike of the new county, which put the
Tyne first in its title and replaced the historic County Durham in postal
addresses. Tyne and Wear County Council was also felt to be run by
Newcastle to its own advantage.

The headquarters were indeed in Newcastle, but the political control
was in fact in the hands of former Labour members of Durham County
Council from areas now included in the South Tyneside and Gateshead
areas of the new county, rather than councillors from Newcastle, or
Sunderland. It also reflected the fact that neither Sunderland nor Newcastle
sent top-tier leading Labour councillors to serve on Tyne and Wear. The
chief executive was Jim Gardner, who moved to that post from Sunderland,
along with several other chief officers.

There were good arguments for linking Sunderland with the
Metropolitan Districts on Tyneside. All experienced the same problems of
urban conurbations with declining industries. There was also a case for
certain major economic and transport decisions being taken at a higher
level than the individual local authorities and these two areas were among
the County's priorities, along with the development of cultural and tourism
policies.

There were, however, to be major problems with two separate planning
and engineering departments involved in projects. These conflicts did not
exist where the County Council was responsible for distinct services, such
as public transport, the regional Newcastle Airport, the fire brigade, the
probation services and consumer protection; the police in Tyne and Wear
County were combined with that of Northumberland to create the
Northumbria force. The County also took the lead in the regional bodies

concerned with culture and tourism as well as directly running museums.

The Borough of Sunderland continued to be responsible for the majority of the services which had most direct impact on the public such as education, housing, social services, leisure, libraries, refuse collection and local planning and highways. As a 'metropolitan district' it operated a wider range of services than would have been the case if it had been one of the 'shire districts' within County Durham. Their education and social service provision, for instance, was decided at County Council level.

One grievance of Sunderland people about the County Council was the Metro rapid transport system, inaugurated in 1980, which was one of Tyne and Wear's main priorities. Because the old Tyneside Passenger Transport Authority had planned it in the early 1970s, the Metro served every Tyne and Wear District apart from Sunderland. As Sunderland was the largest District in the County, however, it paid the largest amount to the County's budget and thus to the Metro. The fact that Tyne and Wear County subsidised the railway link to Newcastle and buses in Sunderland and also introduced an integrated transport policy with through ticketing, as well as through transport for pensioners across Tyne and Wear, did not seem to be adequate compensation.

Economic development was a major objective and Sunderland undoubtedly benefited from its outstanding success in the industrial field. The County, and in particular Jim Gardner, played a key role in the partner-

A 'Pacer' diesel railbus passes Monkwearmouth Station Museum in February 1986; this was one of six units purchased by Tyne and Wear County Council for use on the Sunderland-Newcastle line. For a short period in 1986 most trains, buses and Metrocars operating within the County were painted in this Tyne and Wear Transport yellow and white livery and branding, but this ceased for buses after deregulation of services later in the year.

ship with the Borough and the Washington Development Corporation which was successful in bringing the Nissan motor plant to Washington. Other economic policies included helping to finance the Port of Sunderland through the joint authority with the Borough.

There was little regret on Wearside when the County Council was abolished in 1986 and its powers given to the Borough Council, which was once again the only local government body for Sunderland. Some of the County's functions, such as the fire brigade and museums, remained with joint bodies representing the five district councils. There has continued to be co-operation between them on general economic and other matters, a process helped by the fact that until 2002 all were under Labour control.

The abolition of the County Council meant that strategic issues of planning and development returned to the Borough Council. At the same time the Washington Development Corporation was being wound up and its responsibilities were transferred to the Borough. From 1987 the Borough had, however, to share power again when the responsibility for the regeneration of most of the riverbanks up to North Hylton passed to a new government quango, the Tyne and Wear Development Corporation.

The Council retained its key role in the economic development of all the other areas of Sunderland. In the 1980s a start was made on the planning of Doxford International Business Park in conjunction with the private sector. The importance of this, and of employment creation generally, showed how far economic development had moved up the Council agenda since 1967 when there was only one, purely advisory, Industrial Development Officer at a fairly low level in the local authority.

Housing

The rate of council house building in Sunderland slowed down after the Conservatives came to power in 1967. They did, however, continue the policy of clearing areas of Victorian housing. While many of the worst slums had been demolished there were still some serious problems, particularly with rented property. As late as 1971 10 percent of houses in the town were without baths and hot water.

A view about 1970 of a cottage in Hedley Street, Millfield, where houses were locally considered to be in poor condition, but which were not included in the Council's first clearance proposals for the area.

By the late 1960s there was a feeling that houses were being cleared not because they were slums, but because they stood in the way of general 'improvement' and redevelopment of complete areas. Matters came to a head in Millfield in 1967 when it was planned to demolish streets of cottages, many of which were in relatively good condition and were owner occupied. The people living in them did not wish to move to estates on the outskirts of the town where they would be separated from family and friends and lack the social and shopping amenities they had in Millfield. In addition, although Sunderland had built a record number of council houses, they tended to have fewer rooms than the national average and Millfield people did not wish to move to properties where they could not have their families to stay.

The Millfield Residents Association, which was formed at a meeting called by the Revd Jim Taylor, Vicar of St Mark's Church, spearheaded opposition to the proposed demolition in Millfield. The Association's

secretary was Norman Dennis, a sociology lecturer and later a Labour councillor. The group secured a far higher level of public participation in planning decisions than previously. The Millfield campaign was ultimately successful in greatly reducing the number of houses demolished in favour of renovation of existing property.

The last major housing development in the County Borough area was the new estate at Doxford Park, which had a mixture of council and private sector housing and was generally better planned and provided with more amenities than previous estates. The construction of new housing declined in the new Borough as the slum properties had been demolished and the inclusion of Washington New Town in the Borough brought in a

These houses in Wood Street, Millfield, were proposed for demolition when photographed in 1970 (left), but this was one of the proposals successfully resisted by the Millfield Residents' Association. By the 1980s (right) they had been modernised and partially rebuilt.

Argyle Square, seen here about 1970, was one of several Victorian 'gated streets' of terraced houses which were found particularly around the Ashbrooke area.

The Gilley Law flats and maisonettes completed in 1967. They were initially heated by a coal-fired heating system for the estate which was intended to use coal from local pits, although several of these soon closed.

Housing at Doxford Park. Although this estate was better planned than several of its predecessors, there were to be problems with these flat-roofed houses.

new stock of houses. Those, which the Development Corporation owned, came under local authority control in 1980. By then the tenants of council houses were entitled to purchase their properties and the amount of public housing in Sunderland began to fall.

By the 1980s the Council was concentrating on the demolition or improvement of the worst of its housing stock. The three and four-storey maisonettes, such as Barclay Court in Monk-wearmouth, had proved particularly unpopular. Campaigns to improve the council houses were led in the East End, Ford and Southwick by neighbourhood advice centres.

Several co-operative housing associations, most notably the Banks of the Wear, also developed during this period. These took over existing privately owned houses and the former National Coal Board Wearmouth Colliery houses. Other housing associations built sheltered housing for the elderly.

Wearmouth Colliery workers' houses in Southwick Road, which were sold by the National Coal Board to the Banks of the Wear Housing Association. The plaque above the left of the two doors marks where the municipal boundary between Sunderland and Southwick Councils was until 1928.

In 1990 it was proposed to transfer houses in the Downhill, Hylton Castle, Town End Farm and part of Red House estates to a Housing Action Trust. The government promised about £80 million to upgrade the houses, but the proposal was turned down in a ballot of tenants, even though an abstention was counted as a vote in favour of the transfer.

Education

The process of introducing comprehensive education in the Borough was completed in the early 1970s when the last of the secondary modern schools disappeared. The secondary schools now included Ryhope, which had come into the County Borough in 1967. Here Ryhope Grammar and Secondary Modern Schools were amalgamated to become a single comprehensive in 1969. The new head was Dick Copland, who had clear policies on issues such as extending mixed stream teaching as far as possible and abolishing corporal punishment. These did not accord with the more traditional educational views of some parents in the mining community of Silksworth. Controversy dogged Ryhope in the late 1970s and early 1980s.

The local government reorganisation of 1974 added many more schools in the Houghton, Hetton and Washington areas, including several new buildings which had been erected in Washington New Town. The construction of new schools continued in Washington, notably with Oxclose Comprehensive, which had a wider community function. New premises also replaced some of the older primary schools in central Sunderland, such as St Mary's and Green Street.

Major changes to Sunderland's secondary school system came in the late 1980s when it was decided to introduce a tertiary system which meant schoolchildren over 16 going to Wearside or Monkwearmouth Colleges rather than staying in their current schools. This was because some comprehensives had extremely small sixth forms and school rolls were generally beginning to fall. The three Catholic secondary schools of St Aidan, St Anthony and St Robert of Newminster in Washington retained their sixth forms. St Thomas Aquinas closed.

The status of Wearside and Monkwearmouth Colleges was greatly enhanced when they became responsible for providing most of Sunderland's post-16 public sector education. This was the culmination of a major expansion and change of role of these two colleges of further education. Wearside, which had replaced West Park in 1971, had continued that college's role in training for the largely male construction and heavy industries. Monkwearmouth dealt with training for jobs such as

Wearside College in Sea View Road West, which replaced West Park College. It was officially opened in 1972 by Margaret Thatcher, then Education Secretary. The building was demolished in the early 2000s and new houses were built on the site.

nursing, secretarial work, baking and tailoring. As many of the traditional industries declined the courses offered, particularly at Wearside, changed markedly.

Monkwearmouth College, which was pioneering new computer courses in the late 1980s, took over the former St Thomas Aquinas Catholic School premises at Red House in 1987; these became its Hylton centre. With the granting of tertiary college status Monkwearmouth became additionally responsible for A level and general vocational education in the north and west of the town. It also acquired the former Shiney Row School which was rebuilt as a centre for arts courses. Wearside College assumed responsibilities for A level and general vocational training in the south of the Borough as well as continuing its automotive and other specialised courses. Wearside also took over the buildings of the former Bede School which, like Ryhope, had closed as part of the secondary education reorganisation.

Two of the three colleges of higher education – the Technical College and the College of Art – joined together in 1969 as Sunderland Polytechnic with the College of Education becoming part of the same institution in 1975. The Polytechnic developed many degree courses, in education, general arts and science subjects as well as in specialised subjects such as glass design. Its Chester Road campus particularly expanded during the 1970s and 1980s.

While the Polytechnic pioneered sandwich courses for local students it increasingly attracted students from throughout Britain and from overseas. The numbers of students expanded from 2,300 full-time and sandwich course students in 1980 to 9,500 in 1990. In 1989 the Polytechnic became a Higher Education Corporation independent of the local authority.

The Town Centre

Sunderland's new pedestrianised town centre development was opened in 1969. It reflected the planning and architectural tastes of its time. At ground level were 77 shops, a new Jacky White's Market and a bus station. The first floor, with its concrete walkways linking all sides also had entrances to some commercial premises. Above were a multi-storey car park and three 19-storey blocks of flats – Astral, Planet and Solar Houses. In 1977 the Crowtree Leisure Centre, one of the country's largest indoor sports and recreation centres, was opened on the opposite side of Crowtree Road to the shopping centre.

The Crowtree Leisure Centre under construction in 1976. The roof was constructed on the ground and then raised and the walls of the building were constructed below it. A former Corporation bus, now in Tyne and Wear PTE livery, is about to turn into the Central Bus Station.

The town centre development was notorious for its wind tunnels, which caused problems for shoppers, and it soon began to look outdated after Newcastle's Eldon Square undercover shopping centre was opened in the mid-1970s. Sunderland followed suit 10 years later and the town centre shopping centre was covered in and greatly upgraded. It reopened as the Bridges undercover shopping development in 1988, but by this date Sunderland was beginning to be adversely affected by the vast MetroCentre development on the outskirts of Gateshead, which could be

An aerial view of the town centre in 1969 with the new pedestrianised shopping precinct in the centre being dominated by the three 19-storey blocks of flats and the multi-storey car park. The St Mary's Way section of the inner ring road is under construction on the left.

easily reached by train or bus. An ominous sign for the future was when House of Fraser closed Binns' east (furniture and food) store in Fawcett Street after it opened the MetroCentre shop which took over the position of its flagship store in the North-East.

The opening of the town centre development in 1969 moved the town's commercial heart westwards and contributed to the decline of the lower end of High Street West and Fawcett Street. The status of Fawcett Street took another major blow when the Town Hall was demolished following the opening of the new Civic Centre on West Park in 1970. The Town Hall was hastily demolished in 1971 to meet the deadline for obtaining grants

Fawcett Street about 1972 with an Economic bus passing the hoarding surrounding the former reading rooms which had been demolished along with the Town Hall. The Sunderland Building Society, whose offices lay to the left of the lamppost, had recently amalgamated to form the Sunderland and South Shields Society.

for the construction of a new hotel on the site. The hotel was never built and the site remained vacant for several years, aggravating the annoyance of many people about the loss of the much-loved local landmark.

The suburban shopping centres began to decline markedly during the 1970s and 1980s with branches of national and local grocery chains closing along with local branches of banks. The centres in the towns, which came into Sunderland in 1974 – Houghton, Hetton and Washington Concord – also saw a lesser decline.

One of the most noticeable cutbacks in a shopping chain was that of the Co-ops, many of which were running at a loss by the mid-1960s, particularly as collieries in the pit villages ceased production. Sunderland Co-op took over its Ryhope and Silksworth counterpart in 1967. Sunderland Co-op's chief executive, David Hughes, introduced new ideas. The branch at Castletown became an American one-stop shop with a crèche for

The Grand Hotel in Bridge Street, once Sunderland's principal hotel, after its closure in 1969. This left the Mowbray Park as the only hotel in the town centre. Various plans for a new hotel, such as on the Town Hall site, failed to bear fruit until the Travelodge was opened in 2003.

A group of shops in Hylton Road in 1970. This was one of the shopping centres which declined during the 1970s and 1980s. William Duncan was a South Shields-based grocery firm that was later taken over by Fine Fare.

David Goldman's jewellers and pawnbrokers shop in Rutland Street in 1970. This disappeared during the redevelopment of this section of Millfield. The number of pawnbrokers declined during the second half of the 20th century.

children, but the Co-op had neither the sites nor money to keep up with its competitors. The formation of the North Eastern Co-operative Society in 1970 brought economies of scale, but it barely stemmed the tide of closures which included the main stores at Sunderland and Ryhope. By the end of the century there were only four Co-op stores left in the Borough.

Washington New Town

It was ironic that Sunderland Council had been the main objector to the designation of Washington New Town in 1964 because it feared the effects on its own development. From 1974 Washington greatly benefited the new Borough by providing greenfield sites for new industries, with additional

These receipts were issued by leading town centre stores during the 1960s–80s (Disco were the Co-op). By the end of the 1990s all had vanished.

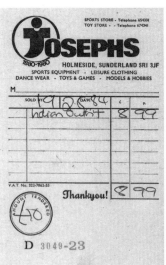

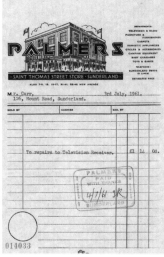

grants available from the Development Corporation. It also added a range of public housing.

The Master Plan envisaged the establishment of 18 'villages', of mixed housing with their own amenities, and 10 industrial estates. By 1982 16,820 houses of a wide variety of types had been built in the New Town; 10,588 were for rent. The Development Corporation had built the vast majority of these houses; its stock was transferred to the Borough Council in 1980. The population of 20,000 in the existing settlements in the area in 1964 grew to 55,000 in 1987.

The town centre was established at the Galleries, a two-deck shopping and business centre. It succeeded in attracting Woolco and Savacentre stores in addition to smaller shops; a new library, sports centre and health centre were also provided there. Leisure facilities were also provided outside the town centre area with the Northumbria Sports Centre, sports fields, new parks and the Washington Wildfowl Park.

The most important achievement of the Washington Development

Looking east over the Galleries shopping centre under construction in the new town centre of Washington towards Glebe Village. Beyond the houses are the spoil heaps and buildings of Glebe Colliery, closed in 1973.

The two-level Galleries shopping and business centre in Washington. Linked to the Galleries were a bus station, library, sports centre and health centre.

The actress Pat Phoenix ('Elsie Tanner' from *Coronation Street*) and Sunderland Football Club players Ian Porterfield (right) and Vic Hallom (left) open the Woolco department store in Washington on 30 May 1973. This store subsequently closed and is now Asda.

Corporation was the commerce and industry it attracted to the area. These included the main Post Office parcels distribution centre for the North-East, printing, light engineering and warehousing. The Child Benefit Centre was a further important source of employment. Most important of all was the siting of the Nissan plant in Washington.

Transport

From the 1960s car ownership increased in Sunderland, although it remained well below the national average. The need to cater for the greater movement of cars and lorries led to the construction of St Mary's Way as the first stage of the inner ring road system which was completed in the 1990s. Further out a series of new roads led from Ryhope Toll Bar to Durham Road. The most significant development for removing through traffic from the town centre was the completion in 1974 of the section of the A19 which bypassed the town to the west and crossed the Wear over a new bridge between North and South Hylton.

The introduction of single deck one-person buses, in place of the double deckers with a driver and conductor, continued from 1966. The flat fare system was ended by the Council on financial grounds in 1969 and replaced by a zonal system which divided Sunderland into three zones.

The Hylton Bridge carrying the A19 Sunderland bypass over the Wear between North and South Hylton was opened in 1974. Like the Chartershaugh Bridge of 1975 further west which carries the Washington Highway over the Wear it is a box girder structure.

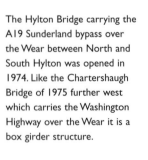

In 1973 Sunderland Corporation Transport passed to the Passenger Transport Executive, which already covered Tyneside. It was renamed the Tyne and Wear Passenger Transport Executive in 1974 when it came under the control of the new County Council. The PTE had a co-ordinating role for all public transport. As well as directly operating the former Corporation bus services it also specified the pattern of services and the fares charged on the bus services of the northern group of companies in Tyne and Wear as well as the trains on the Sunderland to Newcastle line. The frequency of the train service on this route increased, ultimately, to every 15 minutes, while that of the route south of the town declined to every hour.

A high speed train on the early morning Newcastle to London service which ran via Sunderland and Middlesbrough from 1983. There was a return train in the evening, but both ceased in the early 1990s.

One of the Tyne and Wear Passenger Transport Executive's achievements was the development of an integrated transport system with through ticketing between the different bus operators, the trains to Newcastle and, on Tyneside, the Metro and ferry services. Most of this was lost, however, when the government policy of deregulating bus services, to encourage competition between the different bus companies, was introduced in 1986. There was in fact little direct competition between Busways (the former PTE buses) and Northern, both of whom were soon privatised. Smaller competitors were gradually squeezed out.

Sunderland Central Bus Station in October 1986, a few days before the deregulation of bus services. The Tyne and Wear Passenger Transport Executive had replaced the former Corporation single deck buses with double deck vehicles, but after deregulation the process was reversed again.

Twenty-Five Years of Change

Looking back from 1991 over the previous 25 years many Sunderland folk felt that old certainties had disappeared. The Council was no longer the only organisation deciding Sunderland's future. The period also saw the end of several of Sunderland's traditional industries, including, almost unbelievably, shipbuilding.

The end of shipbuilding had a greater impact on the town than the numbers employed in the yards in its final years would have suggested. This was undoubtedly because it was the industry for which Sunderland was best known. In addition the gaps left by the closed shipyards were visible to everyone crossing the Wearmouth and Queen Alexandra Bridges. Resentment about the loss of yards which were among the most modern in

Margaret Thatcher at the official opening of the Nissan factory on 8 September 1986. The first Bluebird car had come off the production line on 8 July; it is now on display in Sunderland Museum. The Bluebird was followed by the Primera and Micra models.

Charles Slater, the long-serving leader of Sunderland Council, who resigned in 1990 after being deselected by his ward party. He recalls that after his resignation he received a note of thanks from the Labour Group on a sheet torn off a pad, a letter 'signed on behalf of the Chief Executive' – and the present of a book from the Liberal Councillors!

Europe continued and morale in the town undoubtedly suffered. For some this seemed more important than the city's success in attracting new industries, most notably the Nissan car plant.

September 1990 saw the fall from power of two once powerful political leaders. Margaret Thatcher resigned as Prime Minister and Charles Slater resigned as Leader of Sunderland Council. They had respectively dominated national and local politics for years. Margaret Thatcher was disliked by many people on Wearside where she was associated with the harsh economic policies of the 1980s that had seen the end of shipbuilding and the defeat of the miners in 1984. The government she led had nonetheless given major support to the establishment of Nissan on Wearside.

Charles Slater had been a major political figure since he became chairman of the Planning Committee in 1961 and had been Leader of the Council for 16 of the 18 years since Labour returned to power in 1972; the gap was during and immediately after he was Mayor. It is worth noting that in addition to his political role Slater had a full-time job as a solicitor.

In the 1980s Charles Slater ensured the Council group kept on a centrist course in spite of the left controlling the District and Constituency parties. Other Labour councils in the region had experienced a far greater degree of internal disagreements and splits.

The political stability in Sunderland at time of great change was one of Charles Slater's legacies. It stands alongside his roles in securing the town centre redevelopment, comprehensive and tertiary education and Nissan, which he himself viewed as the main achievements of a long political career.

CHAPTER 4

The City of Sunderland 1992–2003

The City Council

1992 was a landmark year in the history of Sunderland. In this year the town was granted city status and the Polytechnic became a University. The new city was created to mark the 40th anniversary of the Queen's accession and Sunderland was selected from 22 applicants. The enhanced status was undoubtedly a psychological boost for a community which had seen

The banners which appeared on the front of the Museum building, and also on the Wearmouth Bridge, on 14 February 1992 marked the announcement that the Queen had conferred city status on Sunderland.

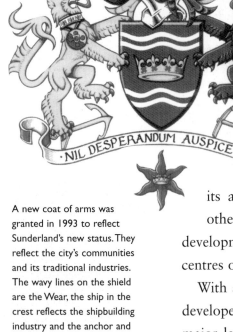

massive upheavals in the previous 20 years. To Wearsiders it was also seen as long overdue recognition that Sunderland was the largest local authority between Leeds and Edinburgh. To reflect Sunderland's new city status St Michael's, Bishop-wearmouth Parish Church, became Sunderland Minster in 1998.

The role and working of the City Council, as it now became, underwent changes during the decade from 1992, with economic regeneration taking an even higher profile, usually in conjunc-tion with other public and private sector partners. By the early 1990s it was clear that the city's economic future would depend not only on Nissan and its associated automotive companies, but also the call centres and other information technology-based businesses and the University developments that were being planned. Most of these were in the new centres of employment that were being established in the city.

A new coat of arms was granted in 1993 to reflect Sunderland's new status. They reflect the city's communities and its traditional industries. The wavy lines on the shield are the Wear, the ship in the crest reflects the shipbuilding industry and the anchor and pick under the supporting lions, the maritime and coal industries. The lions' collars depict George Stephenson's Hetton Railway (left) and the stars from the Washington Crest (right) while the two roundels hanging from the collar represent Houghton-le-Spring.

With a new economic base emerging as well as city status the Council developed a wider vision for Sunderland. It was responsible for several major leisure and cultural developments including the new City Library and Arts Centre in the former Binns East building in Fawcett Street, the refurbished and extended Museum and Winter Gardens and restored Mowbray Park and the Raich Carter Sports Centre in Hendon. In the Coalfields area the Hetton Centre, opened in 2003, was a multi-purpose building which not only included a new library and sports centre and a learning centre, but also the contact points for several other Council and other public services. This was the start of the 'peoplefirst' programme of bringing a number of Council and other public services under one roof in area centres.

Recognition of the City Council's record came in 2002 when Sunderland was named as one of only 22 'excellent' councils in England. The gov-ernment's Comprehensive Performance Assessment recorded that the local authority has 'a record of significant achievement' and 'a clear and ambit-ious vision for a future of continuous change and improvement'.

The Labour Party retained its commanding lead on Sunderland Council into the 21st century. There were, however, more frequent changes in the leading figures than in previous years. This was especially so after the numerous committees were replaced with a single Cabinet whose members were responsible for different areas of the local authority's work, and

The Queen and the Duke of Edinburgh talk to winners of Golden Jubilee art competition in the entrance to the Museum and Winter Gardens on 7 May 2002. The others in the photograph include (from left) Nigel Sherlock, Lord Lieutenant of Tyne and Wear, the author, Senior Curator of Sunderland Museums, and Colin Sinclair, Chief Executive of the City of Sunderland. Colin Sinclair was Chief Executive from 1993 to 2003 and played a significant role in raising the profile of the city through the major developments of the 1990s and early 2000s.

Councillors competed for the fewer remaining posts with real responsibility.

A possible threat to Labour control of the city came when a ballot took place in October 2001 on whether an elected mayor should be responsible for running Sunderland. This was rejected on Wearside. In the three local authorities in the North-East where voters accepted the post of elected mayor the Labour party was unsuccessful in the subsequent elections.

Continuing Industrial and Commercial Change

Some of Sunderland's traditional industries still remained, but some were in terminal decline. Deep mining in the Durham Coalfield ceased in 1993 when Wearmouth Colliery closed. Not only did this mean the loss of 670

Souvenir ticket to commemorate the launch of the Sunderland Metro Extension by the Queen on 7 May 2002. The Queen inaugurated the Metro after officially opening the Winter Gardens at the start of her Golden Jubilee tour of the North-East.

This view south from Astral House, one of the 1960s town centre flats, was taken in 1991. The original Technical College building of 1901 is in the foreground while other Polytechnic buildings are on the right. The Royal Infirmary, with its tall heating chimney, is in the centre.

jobs in the pit, but it also led to the end of coal trains from Sunderland and the closure of the city's railway motive power depot and administrative offices.

Coal mining was one of the oldest industries to disappear. Glassmaking still continued with Pyrex and studio glass workshops, though Hartley Wood, which had an international reputation for its stained glass, closed, however, in 1997.

Some of the closures which took place during this period were caused by multi-national companies transferring their production abroad. The most notable examples of this were when Grove closed the former Coles Cranes factory in 1998 and Federal Mogul closed the former Hepworth and Grandage piston ring factory in 2002. Both concerns had once been leaders in their fields in Europe.

Other major firms continued to manufacture in the city, but reduced their workforce. Dewhirst, the clothing manufacturer, had been a major source of female employment from the 1970s. Now they scaled down their operation because Marks and Spencer, to whom they were a long-standing supplier, sourced more of their goods from cheaper factories abroad.

One of the most keenly felt losses in Sunderland was as a result of a decision taken by a Sunderland-based company. Sir Paul Nicholson stepped down as chief executive of Vaux in 1998, but remained as chairman. He resigned in 1999 when, against his advice, the Vaux board decided to close the Sunderland and Sheffield breweries. This was in spite of the offer to purchase the breweries made by a management team led by Frank

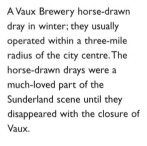

A Vaux Brewery horse-drawn dray in winter; they usually operated within a three-mile radius of the city centre. The horse-drawn drays were a much-loved part of the Sunderland scene until they disappeared with the closure of Vaux.

Nicholson. Sir Paul and many others felt the figures used to justify closure of the breweries were wrong. The Sunderland brewery closed in June 1999 and by the end of the year Vaux had vanished completely, with the public houses being sold to Pubmaster and the Swallow Hotels to Whitbread.

In contrast to the decline of the traditional industries Sunderland became the country's fastest growing automotive centre, centred around Nissan, employing 12,000 people by 2003 – 5,000 of these were in Nissan itself, the largest British carmaker and the most productive car plant in Europe. Between 1986 and 2002 it produced three million cars.

Other Wearside-based companies continue to expand. The Cowie Group, which changed its name to Arriva in 1997, concentrated on developing its passenger transport operations. It became one of the three biggest bus operators in Britain, with over 6,000 buses and the operator of the railway franchises serving the north-east of England and Wales. On the Continent it operates buses in Italy, the Netherlands, Spain and Sweden and trains in Denmark and the Netherlands. It also has a major vehicle hiring operation.

Arriva sold the Cowie vehicle dealerships and leasing arm. In contrast, the Reg Vardy group continued to expand its motor dealerships, becoming the third largest motor retailer in the UK with a turnover of £1.3 billion in 2000. Like Arriva, it moved its headquarters to Doxford International Business Park.

The Solar Office at Doxford International Business Park was one of the most environmentally advanced office buildings in Europe when it was built in the late 1990s. This is the most striking building in the Business Park which has become one of the region's most significant employment centres.

Regenerating the City

Sunderland City Council played the leading role in the economic regeneration of Sunderland. Its most notable achievements, in conjuction with the private sector, were the establishment of the Doxford International Business Park and the redevelopment of the city centre. In other areas the lead was taken by quangos which were set up to administer government funding for specific areas of the city. There were inevitably strains in the relationships between the Council and these bodies.

The City of Sunderland Partnership, which was set up in 1994 to establish Sunderland as a rapidly developing city and the advanced manufacturing centre of the north showed the range of organisations involved along with the City Council. They included the City of Sunderland Training and Enterprise Council, the University of Sunderland, the Tyne and Wear Development Corporation and the Tyne and Wear Chamber of Commerce. Further players were English Estates (later English Partnerships) and the Northern Development Company, which was

Sunderland Marina with the Marine Activities Centre in the centre background. This development of the former North Dock was one of the Tyne and Wear Development Corporation's projects on Wearside.

superseded in 1999 when the government established One North East as the regional development agency.

The Tyne and Wear Development Corporation, which existed between 1988 and 1998, was responsible for the major regeneration of the river banks on the north of the Wear. The Corporation was provided with planning powers and funding to create an environment to attract private sector investment. The chairman was Sir Paul Nicholson of Vaux. In Sunderland their three flagship projects were the Sunderland Enterprise Park at Hylton Riverside, the new Stadium of Light for Sunderland Football Club, which was built on the site of Wearmouth Colliery and the developments in the North Dock and North Sands areas. These comprised a marina and 500 houses and the St Peter's Campus for the University which included the National Glass Centre as well as academic buildings.

Hylton Riverside was one of two Enterprise Zones in Sunderland which offered incentives such as a rates holiday and a streamlined planning process for firms to move in. The other zone, Doxford International Business Park, was administered by the City and was to become the most important site for the economic regeneration of Wearside in the 1990s. It indeed became the most successful enterprise zone in the country employing 7,500 people by 2002. It is where firms, such as Barclays Bank, T Mobile and London Electricity deal with customer enquiries by phone and computer. In addition major firms, such as Arriva, Nike, Northern Rock and Reg Vardy have their offices at Doxford International. By 2003 the Doxford site was full and preparatory work began on the Rainton Bridge South Business Park to attract further financial services and information technology sector jobs.

A further government-funded organisation from 1993 to 1998 was Sunderland City Challenge which was set up to reduce the high rate of unemployment and improve the environment of north-west Sunderland. Its main achievements were often in conjunction with other organisations, such as the Training and Enterprise Council who established the Business and Enterprise Centre at Hylton Riverside. The tight boundaries in which it could work caused problems. Further City Challenge funding went into the more deprived areas of the south of Sunderland. By the late 1990s the additional targeted government support came through the Single Regeneration Budget administered through the City Council.

Following the closure of Coles and Vaux another organisation was set up to help the regeneration of not only the Docks and riverbanks, but also the city centre and particularly the Sunniside area. This was the Sunderland ARC (Area Regeneration Company) established in 2002. It has ambitious plans, particularly on the south bank of the Wear which saw little input from the Tyne and Wear Development Corporation, but in 2003 its impact on the city remains to be seen.

Sunderland's hospitals saw major changes during this period as the decision to concentrate most services on the General Hospital site in Chester Road and close the Royal Infirmary was made. A series of major new buildings were erected at what became known as the Sunderland Royal Hospital and the City Hospitals received recognition as one of the best performing hospitals in the country.

The City Centre and the Shopping Centres

In 1992 the city centre experienced a major blow when the final section of Binns department store closed down. The business had been declining for some years as specialist sections, such as the food hall, were phased out and it undoubtedly suffered as House of Fraser adopted a standard approach to its stores. Jopling's, the other local department store, which took more account of the local market, continued to flourish.

The growth of the Gateshead MetroCentre was another factor which affected not only Binns, but also other Sunderland stores as Wearside people chose to travel to the large new shopping complex. The food retailers in the city centre were also affected by the supermarkets of Asda in Grangetown, Morrison's in Doxford Park and Seaburn, and Sainsbury's in Silksworth Lane. Further competition came from the retail parks at Monkwearmouth, Pallion and Trimdon Street, which included major suppliers of electrical and other household goods and 'do it yourself' stores.

The Park Lane Interchange, which opened in 1999, replaced both the former northern bus station on the same site and the central bus station and also included a Metro station opened in 2002. The architecture is impressive, but it is a very windy place in which to wait for a bus! The large crane towering over the skyline was being used in building the extension to the Bridges Shopping Centre.

To extend the choice offered in the centre of Sunderland the Bridges shopping centre was doubled in size by extending into the former bus station and Crowtree Road. Opened in 2000 the £45-million extension provided a second department store, Debenhams, and other smaller units which were taken up by national retailers, particularly in the clothing sector.

A major part of the revamp of the city centre was the construction of the Park Lane Interchange. This replaced both the bus station previously on the site and the central bus station; it also provided a station for the Metro extension to Sunderland which opened in 2002 and brought people from the suburbs and centre of Newcastle to the city centre. In contrast to the impressive Park Lane Interchange was the fate of Sunderland's railway station. After privatisation of the railway system Railtrack built shops over the only area which allowed daylight on to the platforms, but failed to carry out any improvements for passengers. This left Sunderland with almost certainly the worst city railway station in the country, without any basic facilities such as toilets, a bookstall or a sandwich shop.

The City Council was closely involved in planning the shopping and transport developments in the city centre and was directly responsible for the new City Library and Arts Centre, opened in the former Binns east building in 1997, and for the Mowbray Gardens project completed in 2001. The latter comprised the extension and complete refurbishment of the Museum, the construction of the new Winter Gardens and the restoration of Mowbray Park. A further development in the cultural field came in 2003 when plans were finalised for the refurbishment of the Empire to improve its facilities to take larger touring shows.

A feature of the 1990s was the decline in the number of firms' offices in the city centre. Northern Rock, which took over the North of England Building Society (incorporating the Sunderland and South Shields Society), moved its Sunderland administrative offices to Doxford International, although in this case its building was taken over by the city's social services department. The Sunderland and South Shields Water Company became part of the larger Northumbrian Water based near Durham and its Sunderland offices were left unoccupied for several years. There were also several vacant buildings in the Sunniside area including the Royal Mail's sorting office. In 2003 plans were being drawn up for the regeneration of

the Sunniside area, which involved converting several of the vacant buildings to residential use.

Beyond Sunniside restoration of the group of historic buildings around High Street East took place, notably the Exchange Building which became a restaurant and conference venue. The restoration of this, like that of the Museum and Winter Gardens and Mowbray Park and of Fulwell Windmill was greatly assisted by support from the Heritage Lottery Fund.

Several premises on the western edge of the city centre, such as the original Technical College, were converted to wine bars, pubs or night clubs, as Sunderland's 'night-time economy' developed. Sunderland was, however, without a cinema for several years and it was only in 2003 that a start was made on building a new multi-screen cinema.

The development of supermarkets affected the suburban shopping centres as well as the city centre with Hendon, Grangetown and Hylton Road being particularly badly hit. The Galleries has continued to be the shopping centre for Washington, but the Gateshead MetroCentre has halted the possibility of further major expansion there. Redevelopment also took place in the centre of Houghton, including a new Co-operative supermarket and a new library.

Transport

Sunderland has always had a lower than average level of car ownership, but this rose markedly during the 1990s. Congestion became more of a

Newbottle Street in Houghton-le-Spring showing the Library on the left with the Sunderland Housing Group's offices beyond. These new buildings contrast with the traditional ironmonger's shop on the right. Houghton has managed to retain a viable shopping centre.

On 1 July 1995, the final day of the company's operations, a Jolly bus waits to depart from South Hylton where the company had based its operation for 73 years; the following day the route to Sunderland via Hylton Road was taken over by Stagecoach.

Metrocars at University Station, close to the Chester Road Campus of Sunderland University in 2002, the year the Metro extension to Sunderland and South Hylton opened. This was the route of the former Pensher branch line which had once carried many coal trains as well as a passenger service to Durham. It had been landscaped as a foot and cycle path and had to be rebuilt for the Metro.

A Transpennine service to Liverpool waits in the sidings to enter Sunderland station to take up a service to Liverpool on the first day of operation of this service on 2 June 1996. These sidings are now the route of the Metro extension to South Hylton.

problem in the city centre, although the inner ring road system was extended during the 1990s and the major St Mary's car park was opened.

The Council lacked any control over the now-privatised bus services. Busways, the former Passenger Transport Executive fleet which had been sold to its management and employees in 1989, was taken over by the transport giant, Stagecoach, in 1994. The other major operators were Northern buses, which had been bought out by a management team which now traded locally as Go North East and, to a smaller extent, the United buses, ultimately purchased by Arriva. Almost all the smaller firms were squeezed out by the big three companies.

The railway services to Sunderland were privatised in 1997, being first franchised to MTL and then to Sunderland's Arriva; the infrastructure had already passed to Railtrack. There were problems about the reliable operation of the service during the late 1990s. The main improvement to rail services of the last years of British Rail, the Trans Pennine through trains to Yorkshire and Merseyside, were withdrawn in 2004 when these were let to a new franchisee.

The major transport development on Wearside was in fact provided by one of the few operators to remain in the public sector – the Tyne and Wear Metro. In 2002 the Queen officially opened the Metro extension to Sunderland. This involved connecting the existing Metro system at Pelaw to the railway line to Sunderland, which was electrified and fitted with signalling to allow both Metro and main line trains to run on it. New stations were built in the city at the Stadium of Light and St Peter's and, on the section of the former route to

Durham, at Park Lane Interchange, University, Millfield, Pallion and South Hylton.

Housing

The emphasis of the Council's housing policy during the 1990s was on the refurbishment of its existing stock of houses. Sometimes this could be funded from grants for specific areas, but often had to be financed from capital spending which had to be approved by government. This was a factor in the decision to transfer the Council's houses to the Sunderland Housing Group in 2000.

The Housing Group, the third largest social landlord in the United Kingdom, was able to borrow finance for refurbishment on the financial market. It embarked on refurbishing existing houses and on building the first new houses in the rented sector for over quarter of a century. The Group also had a wider remit than the local authority and started on the conversion of existing buildings in the Sunniside area to provide luxury apartments for sale.

Private rented accommodation in Sunderland was concentrated in the

This view of Hendon in 2003 shows the 1960s flats which, like most of the tower blocks in Sunderland, had been refurbished. The two-storey houses in the foreground are typical of the houses built in Hendon in the 1980s and 1990s.

areas of the town close to the town centre, such as Hendon. It was here that problems arose, especially about the quality of some of the housing and the behaviour of anti-social tenants.

The construction of houses for sale continued throughout the 1990s and early 2000s. Some were in new estates in the outer areas of the city, such as Shiney Row and Washington. New houses were also built on brownfield sites, such as the Public Works depot in Eden Vale, and on large gardens in existing suburban areas. A notable development from the

Willow Green, a block of flats built on the edge of Ashbrooke Sports Ground. This was one of several built in the area in the early 2000s. Even the gap between the two sections of the West Lawn houses seen on the side of the ground was about to be filled up with new construction. The spire of St John's Methodist Church is on the left.

late 1990s was the building of several low-rise blocks of flats, particularly in the Ashbrooke area.

In the years after World War Two the last of the houses close to the Wear had been demolished. From the 1990s housing began to return to the river banks with the North Haven development at the North Dock, student flats at Panns Bank and luxury flats at Bonner's Field.

Education

The policy of local management of schools devolved several of the responsibilities of the Local Education Authority, but it still had to deal with the problem of falling pupil numbers and decisions on which schools to close. It also oversaw the replacement of some of the Victorian primary schools by new buildings. In addition new buildings were constructed for Sandhill View, which also house community facilities. The Venerable Bede, a completely new secondary school, was opened in 2003 on the former Ryhope golf course, in conjunction with the Church of England.

In 1992 Sunderland Church High School for Girls and Tonstall House, a boys' school, merged under the name of Sunderland High School. This created a significant co-educational independent school in the city. A new junior school was opened in Ashbrooke Road and the senior school expanded into several properties adjacent to its main building which were vacated by the University. In 2003 the High School had 610 pupils. The other private schools in the city were Argyle House and Grindon Hall (formerly Fulwell Grange) Christian School.

Monkwearmouth and Wearside Colleges moved out of local authority control in 1993 after which their funding came directly from the Further Education Funding Council. More change came in 1996 when they amalgamated to form the City of Sunderland College, the UK's fifth largest further education college.

The college concentrated teaching on the Bede Centre and new buildings of the Hylton and Shiney Row Centre with the former Wearside College site being sold for housing. In addition to the sixth form provision for many of Sunderland's students, the college provided a wide range of computing and business technology courses. Some were related specifically to call centres; other vocational courses included catering, hairdressing and motor vehicle studies.

In 2003 the College had 27,000 students. Many of these were part time students or adults, often retired, attending a single set of courses. The latter is an area in which the University has also become increasingly involved.

Anne Wright was appointed Rector of Sunderland Polytechnic in 1990 and became the first vice-chancellor in 1992 when the institution became a university, a post she held until 1999. She became the most prominent woman in Sunderland public life.

The University

The Polytechnic, which moved from being part of the local authority to achieving corporate status in 1989, was granted university status in 1992. The University of Sunderland played a significant part not only in education, but also in the economic development of the city. The University's public profile was also greatly raised, partly thanks to the vice-chancellor, Anne Wright, and the chancellor, Lord Puttnam.

The Sunderland University campus at St Peter's which was constructed on former shipyard land in the second half of the1990s. It included a library, large lecture theatre and business school.

The University began a policy of concentrating its teaching on two sites – the Chester Road Campus and the new St Peter's (from 2003 the Sir Tom Cowie) Campus with other buildings, particularly in the Ashbrooke area, being sold off. St Peter's was a completely new campus, being built on the site of the North Sands Shipyard. In the seven years from 1996, £37 million was invested in constructing several buildings, including a business school, library, and informatics and digital media centres. New student accommodation was built at Panns Bank and Pallion.

The courses taught at the University continued to change to reflect changing employment patterns. Of the courses the Technical College offered in 1945 only pharmacy remained and the only engineering course offered was automotive engineering. Teacher training and art and design, which were the areas covered by the Polytechnic's other two constituent colleges, still remained significant areas of teaching. Many of the courses had, however, developed since the 1960s including glass, in which the University had gained an international reputation, media and business studies, information technology and nursing.

In 2003 Sunderland had almost 15,000 students, 8,800 of whom were full time, 2,000 were from 70 countries overseas. The University was the fifth largest employer in the city and it was estimated that it generated between £51 million and £82 million for the economy of Sunderland.

The City in 2003

Sunderland changed more, both physically and in its economic base, in the years between 1992 and 2003 than it had during any other similar period of time in the previous century. The closure of Vaux and Coles Cranes meant that there was still vacant land which was a reminder of Sunderland's lost industries, but by 2003 new buildings now occupied colliery and shipyard sites. Doxford Industrial Business Park, the University campus and the National Glass Centre at St Peter's, the Stadium of Light, the Winter Gardens, the extension to the Bridges Centre, the Park Lane Interchange and the Royal Hospital were all developments, some with 'landmark buildings', which had changed the face of Sunderland.

Some of these new buildings, notably Doxford Park and the St Peter's Campus, were the centres of the areas of growth in the city's economy which were increasingly based on information technology linked areas. Others, like the Museum and Winter Gardens, which attracted a million visitors in just over two years, were to justify the city's policy of regeneration through culture, sport and tourism.

The census of 2001 showed that while Sunderland continued to have a higher rate of unemployment (4.8 percent) than with the national average (3.4 percent), the gap was far less than in the 1980s. As with some of Sunderland's past sources of employment, there was no guarantee that the new jobs, such as those in call centres, might not move elsewhere in years to come. Nevertheless, at the beginning of the 21st century Sunderland had a more diverse and resilient economic base than for many years before.

The Winter Gardens were designed, like the Park Lane Interchange, by the architects Nappers of Newcastle. As well as being well received by visitors, the Winter Gardens have rapidly become one of the best-known buildings in Sunderland and often appear as a symbol of Sunderland's regeneration.

CHAPTER 5

The Business and Political Communities

Much of the transformation of Sunderland since 1945 has been caused by global economic conditions, changes in British society or national political decisions. Other significant developments have been the result of local entrepreneurship and skills and local political decisions. A relatively small number of industrialists, businessmen and councillors have been responsible for many important changes.

Most of the families whose ancestors had been involved with the growth of the town during the 19th century had left the area by the end of World War Two. In the following years the last of the major Victorian landowners, the Pembertons and the Williamsons, also moved from the area, leaving only the Earls of Durham and the Marquises of Londonderry with their stately homes in County Durham. Even the latter's links with Wearside became more tenuous as the years progressed.

Several of the shipbuilding and shipowning and other leading business and industrial families had also moved from the town, mainly to Whitburn, Cleadon or more distant attractive areas of County Durham and North Yorkshire. This meant that it was often the smaller businessmen who became most involved with the political life of Sunderland.

The most important group of local decision makers in Sunderland since 1945 have been the leading members of the local Labour party. Labour had been involved in municipal politics since the late 19th century, but its period of dominance only began after 1945; it has continued, with only a short break, into the 21st century.

The Business Community

In 1945 much of the town's commercial life was controlled by the families of those who had established the industries and businesses in the 19th century or who had taken over their management in the early 20th century. By the beginning of the 21st century almost none of these families were still

Sir Myers Wayman (1890–1959) was Mayor of Sunderland from 1938 to 1943 and chairman of the town's War Industrial Committee. In addition to his many business interests, he was a magistrate, Deputy Lieutenant for County Durham and a River Wear Commissioner. He was also vice-chairman of the British National Savings Movement.

involved in Wearside commerce. Control of much of Sunderland's commercial and industrial life was in the hands of national or multi-national companies. On the other hand a few notable new local entrepreneurs had established or expanded firms which had branches across the country.

There were many smaller businesspeople in Sunderland who did not gain the national prominence of the town's important industrialists. Some concentrated on running their own businesses. Others were members of the Sunderland Chamber of Commerce and of the (all male) Sunderland Club. Cliques inevitably emerged, one of which in the 1930s and 1940s was apocryphally known in the town as 'The Forty Thieves'. They were reputed to have been involved in various dubious business ventures.

The most prominent Sunderland businessman during the years around World War Two was Sir Myers Wayman, Mayor from 1943 to 1945, whose political career was an example of the link between the Moderates on the Town Council and the commercial community. Wayman's father had been a funeral director, but his own business interests extended far wider. He was chairman of the Sunderland Working Men's Building Society and of Mayfair Products, the confectionery company which owned three factories in Sunderland and interests beyond the town.

Samuel Storey (1898–1978) with members of the Conservative Ladies Tea Club. Storey, a member of the family which had controlled the *Sunderland Echo* from its foundation in 1873, was chairman of the controlling Portsmouth and Sunderland Newspapers company from 1925 to 1973 and also held national posts in the newspaper industry. He was an MP for Sunderland from 1931 to 1945 and later the MP for Stretford before becoming Lord Buckton.

The Major Industrialists

Shipbuilding and ship repairing was the industry that showed best the continuing influence in 1945 of the families of the Victorian founders. Bartram's, Greenwell's Pickersgill's, Short's and Thompson's were all managed by members of the families whose name they bore and Laing's by the Marrs who had a long involvement with that yard. By 1973 they had all left shipbuilding following the takeover by outside interests of the two merged shipbuilding groups – Austin and Pickersgill and Doxford and Sunderland – or closure in the case of Short's.

The careers of many of the 'traditional' managing directors of the shipyards were often remarkably similar. They studied naval architecture, often at Armstrong College, Newcastle, and then worked for a few years at one of the other yards on the Wear before moving to the family firm and becoming directors. Several were presidents of national shipbuilding organisations. Many were members of the River Wear Commissioners and of local companies such as the Sunderland and South Shields Water Company and the Sunderland Working Men's Building Society, served as magistrates and held office in the Conservative Party.

The post-war managing directors owed their positions to their family connections, but some were undoubtedly men of ability. Cyril Thompson, for instance, who was joint managing director of J.L. Thompson in 1940, had led a delegation to the US in 1940 to arrange for the first 'Liberty' ships to be built there. He succeeded his father, Sir Norman Thompson, as chairman of Thompson's in 1951 and during the next few years £1 million was invested in the modernisation of the North Sands Yard. The *Borgsten*, launched in 1963, was the biggest ship to have been built in a British shipyard for many years. Among the posts he held were President of the Shipbuilders Employers Association and President of the North East Institution of Engineers and Shipbuilders.

When Cyril Thompson died suddenly in 1967 he was deputy chairman of the Doxford and Sunderland Engineering Company, of which Thompson's was now part. His son, Patrick, was then general manager of the North Sands yard, but following the takeover of the Doxford and Sunderland Group by the Court Line Company he and the other shipbuilding family members left the industry.

The most notable of the Wearside shipbuilding directors in post-war years was from outside the family firms. Ken Douglas started his career on the Wear at the age of 16 before qualifying as a naval architect. In 1958 he became managing director of Austin & Pickersgill where he developed the

Robert Bartram (1894–1981) started work at the family South Docks shipyard in 1912 when he was on vacation from Armstrong College, Newcastle. After war service he became a director, managing director and then chairman. He oversaw the merger of Bartram and Sons with Austin and Pickersgill before retiring in 1970. In the 1930s he was a Sunderland Town Councillor and was later Chairman of the Bench and Chairman of the River Wear Commissioners and a Director of the Sunderland and South Shields Water Company.

philosophy of a standard design bulk cargo carrier. The SD14 was a hugely successful design and over 200 were built not only on the Wear, but also elsewhere in Britain and abroad.

Ken Douglas's talents were recognised when he was appointed managing director of Upper Clyde Shipbuilders in 1969, but the massive problems of the Scottish yards resulted in the collapse of the company and after a spell with the succeeding Govan Shipbuilders he left the industry in 1973, only to return to British Shipbuilders in 1978. From 1979 to 1983 he was again managing director of Austin and Pickersgill. His name was also unsuccessfully put forward as a potential chairman of the nationalised British Shipbuilders.

Outside the shipbuilding industry there were two major firms in Sunderland, which had grown significantly during the inter-war years due to the skills of two outstanding businessmen. One was James A. Jobling, the glassmakers, where Ernest Jobling-Purser had acquired the rights from Corning in 1921 to manufacture Pyrex heat-resistant glass in Britain and most of the Empire. The American firm had previously been rebuffed by the leading British glass manufacturing firms. Jobling-Purser's connection with Sunderland ceased, however, in 1949 when the company passed out of local control.

The second firm with an outstanding figure in 1945 was Vaux and Associated Breweries where Sir Frank Nicholson had seen a major expansion of the business, including amalgamation with North Eastern Breweries in 1927, which had created the region's second largest brewers. Sir Frank died in 1952 after 54 years involvement with the company, but the Nicholson family's involvement with Vaux continued for a further two generations until the closure of the company in 1999. The Nicholsons only held a fairly small shareholding in Vaux – less than 0.5 percent.

Douglas Nicholson, who succeeded his father as chairman of Vaux, was in turn followed by his son Paul in 1976; both had served the company in various positions including managing director before they became chairmen. Their period of control saw massive expansion of the firm which began after Douglas purchased Ward's brewery in Sheffield and several firms in Scotland, making them the third largest brewers there. The off-licence trade was also expanded following the purchase of the Blayney's off licence chain in 1968. Douglas Nicholson also pioneered sports sponsorship through 'Vaux Encourage Sport'.

The two most significant developments were probably the growth of the national Swallow Hotels chain and the enlargement and modernisation of

Ken Douglas, well-known in Sunderland as 'Mr SD14' after the successful standard design cargo ship he developed while managing director of Austin and Pickersgill. Outside shipbuilding he was chairman of the governors when Sunderland Polytechnic became a University.

Vaux's Sunderland brewery. In 1978 a £2 million investment in the brewery increased capacity by three quarters of a million pints.

In 1997 the Vaux Group employed 9,800 people and had a turnover of £111 million. Yet two years later, as related in the previous chapter, the Group had ceased to exist and the Sunderland brewery closed in spite of a management buy-out offer led by Frank Nicholson, younger brother of Paul, who was managing director of Vaux Breweries.

The members of the Nicholson family involved with brewing played a significant part in the public life in the region. Sir Frank and his son were River Wear Commissioners, with Sir Frank being the chairman. Sir Paul, knighted in 1993, was chairman of the Tyne and Wear Development Corporation, chairman of the Northern Regional Council of the Confederation of British Industries and the first President of the North East Chamber of Commerce. He was also involved with several other North-East organisations and companies. His brother Frank chaired several local organisations, such as the Wearside Opportunity and the City of Sunderland Partnership. Sir Frank, Douglas and Sir Paul were also all involved in Conservative politics in various capacities.

Sir Paul Nicholson, Lord Lieutenant of Durham, (right) and Frank Nicholson, High Sheriff of Durham, with their mother Pauline, widow of Douglas Nicholson, in 1999. Sir Paul and his father and grandfather had also been High Sheriff. The Nicholsons are the last of the old-established Sunderland industrial families to play a major part in the public life of the area.

Post-War Entrepreneurs

Many of Wearside's most successful firms in the second half of the 20th century were built up from relatively small family firms, but such was the scale of industrial change that several of these businesses had vanished by the beginning of the 21st century.

Kenneth Brunton Reed (1914–2003) took over the old-established printing firm of Thomas Reed which was already famous for *Reed's Nautical Almanac*. He was responsible for the growth and diversification of the company into new areas of the printing, packaging and conference business. Thomas Reed celebrated its bicentenary in 1982 as an expanding Sunderland company. Fifteen years later it no longer existed although its maritime titles continued to be published by others.

The Steels Group was an even more spectacular example of the growth and then disappearance of a major Sunderland firm. Sir James Steel joined the firm of builder's merchants founded by his grandfather as an apprentice in 1928 and was to become its sales director and then chairman.

Sir James Steel (1909–1994) on the left with Kenneth Robinson, Minister of Planning in 1964. Sir James was responsible for much of the growth of the Steels Group, whose best-known products were Coles Cranes. In the 10 years from 1946 he visited 90 countries in search of exports. Sir James was the first chairman of the Washington Development Corporation and was Lord Lieutenant of Tyne and Wear from 1974 to 1984.

In 1939 the Steels Group, now a public company, bought the crane making firm of Henry J. Coles of Derby. They also began to build cranes for the forces at the Crown Works in Pallion, which became the largest crane manufacturing works in Europe. In the early days they had to share the premises with the manufacture of Steels' other products, including catering equipment, fireplaces, neon lights, electric vehicles, agricultural machinery, snowploughs and anchors.

Coles Cranes became, with ships and Pyrex, one of Sunderland's best-known products. The business was sold to the Acrow group in 1972, although still with Steel family involvement. This ceased after it later became part of the American Groves operation in 1984. Initially Groves expanded the Pallion Works by moving production from other plants, but in 1998 the Sunderland Works were closed.

One Sunderland firm which grew dramatically from the 1960s and was happily still flourishing at the beginning of the 21st century was Edward Thompson under the chairmanship of Frank Cronin. Thompson's developed from a small stationery and printing business into a major firm which employed 700 people in 2002 in bingo supplies, promotional games, printing, recycled paper making, direct mailing, advertising book and box matches and electronics. They became particularly well known for being the world's largest manufacturer of bingo cards, producing as many as one billion cards a week on many occasions as well as ballot papers for elections in Nigeria and South Africa.

Motor dealerships were a business in which Sunderland became nationally known in the 50 years after World War Two. This was due to two outstandingly successful entrepreneurs – Sir Tom Cowie and Sir Peter Vardy. Tom Cowie had been involved in running his father's motorcycle business as a teenager in the 1930s and, following service in the RAF, reopened the shop in Millfield in 1948 after buying six used motorcycles. In 1952 he opened new premises in Hylton Road and a branch in Newcastle and, taking advantage of the boom in motorcycles and scooters, had branches throughout the North-East and in Edinburgh and Glasgow by 1960.

In the early 1960s, with a declining demand for motorcycles, the firm moved into selling cars and by March 1963 these accounted for 80 percent of Cowie's profits. Throughout the 1960s, 1970s and 1980s the firm expanded into a national group with the acquisition of several major car dealerships and also the development of car leasing so that it became one of the leading car contract hire companies in the world.

Cowie's also developed its own financial arm, Red Dragon Securities, and, most significantly, moved into the passenger transport business with the purchase of Grey-Green Coaches. The drive for this expansion came very much from Sir Tom Cowie until his retirement in 1993, which was followed by the change of the firm's name to Arriva in 1997. Sir Tom has continued his business involvement with Sunderland through his chairmanship of North Eastern Marine Services, based at the South Docks, which specialises in importing aluminum and in metals, bonded and general warehousing. Well-known for his financial support for Sunderland University and for many other local charities, Sir Tom is one of the best

A bingo machine being assembled at the Edward Thompson premises in Richmond Street in the early 1970s. The firm offered a 'bespoke bingo' service covering advice, equipment manufacture, installation and supply of bingo tickets.

Sir Tom Cowie (centre) and Sir Peter Vardy (right) with Professor Peter Fidler, vice-chancellor of Sunderland University, after the opening of the Reg Vardy Centre endowed by Sir Peter. It is part of the Business School on Sunderland University's Sir Tom Cowie Campus, which was named to recognise his major support for development. In addition to being chairman of the University's Development Trust Sir Tom was chairman of Sunderland Football Club between 1980 and 1987. He was also treasurer and then chairman of the Sunderland Conservative Association.

known and respected Sunderland businessmen. Reg Vardy, who established the second of Sunderland's major motor retailers, had started work in 1923 with a horse and cart clearing ashpits and delivering coal with his brother in Houghton-le-Spring. During the 1950s he established car showrooms at Stoneygate on the road to Durham. Peter Vardy took over in 1976 and greatly expanded the successful car retailing business.

By 1982 Reg Vardy held franchises for Rolls-Royce, Aston Martin, Ferrari and Jaguar/Daimler as well the original Ford dealership. In the next 20 years Reg Vardy developed to become the third largest motor retailer in the United Kingdom with 90 dealerships, a turnover of £1.3 billion and 5,000 employees.

Both Sir Tom Cowie and Sir Peter Vardy have been notable philanthropists on a larger scale than Sunderland has seen before. In the 19th century several of the local industrialists and businessmen endowed churches and public facilities, but to a lesser degree than in many other industrial towns. The first major benefactor who gave widely to good causes was Sir John Priestman in the first half of the 20th century. In recent times Sir Tom Cowie has given away £2 million through the Sir Tom Cowie Foundation and served as chairman of the University of Sunderland Development Trust. Sir Peter's Vardy Foundation has been the major sponsor of Emmanuel City Technology College in Gateshead and the King's Academy in Middlesbrough, as well as donating £1 million to the University of Sunderland Business School.

Sir Tom Cowie's and Sir Peter Vardy's businesses excelled in selling motor vehicles. Sunderland has also achieved successes in retailing in other areas. In 2003 for the second year running Simon Heptinstall, chief executive of Storey Carpets, received the National Flooring Industry's Best Retailer of the Year Award for the Washington-based company. Founded in Sunderland in 1921 as a retailer of furniture and other goods the firm grew rapidly during the 1980s and 1990s to become Britain's third largest carpet retailer.

The Leighton Group, which specialises in new technology and communications, was another of the city's successes. Established by Paul Callaghan in one room of his father's accountant's office in Vine Place in 1979, it had grown to be a £5 million international company in 2003 based at Doxford International Business Park. The firm's businesses included publishing, e-marketing, the creation of websites for companies such as British Airways and designing on-line educational systems for organisations such as the Open University.

Storey Carpets branch at Armstrong Retail Park in Washington. The company opened a number of stores in 'out of town' retail parks in the 1980s. Storey's expansion has continued in the 2000s with not only new stores, but also the development of an internet business.

In spite of the marked success of some of Sunderland's entrepreneurs there is a feeling among business and civic leaders at the beginning of the 21st century that more new businesses should have started up in the city. The encouragement of new entrepreneurs, particularly in the field of information and other new technologies, is seen as a priority for the future.

The Conservative Party

As in national politics, there have been close links between the business community and the Conservative Party. Several of the prominent industrialists and businessmen mentioned above were presidents or other office bearers in the Sunderland or North-East Conservative organisations.

The Conservatives controlled Sunderland politics for most of the years between the wars, but their influence declined after 1945 and especially after 1974 when the normally rock-solid Labour mining areas became part of the town. They have nevertheless survived as the second political force in the area and their successes included holding the Sunderland South parliamentary seat for 12 years and controlling the Town Council for five years. They still draw support from the working class, particularly the home-owning skilled artisans, as well as the middle class.

Until the late 1940s the party representing both the Conservatives and Liberals on the Council was the Moderates who, as in many British towns, stated that they were opposed to the introduction of national politics into municipal affairs. Several of the leading Moderates were nevertheless leading members of the Sunderland Conservative Party. They were also prominent local businessmen.

J.D.S. ('Tim') Brown, a Sunderland solicitor, was one of the new breed of Conservative Councillors elected in 1967. After serving as chairman of the General Purposes Committee during the Conservative period of power, he was leader of the Conservative Opposition Group from 1979 to 1983.

William Martin (second from the right), a leading Sunderland businessman, first served on the Council from 1934 to 1948. He was then the Conservative Chairman of the Finance Committee from 1967 to 1971 and Mayor during 1972 to 1973. He later became deputy leader of the Conservative group on Tyne and Wear County Council and was a Deputy Lieutenant for Tyne and Wear.

By the time the Conservatives gained power in 1967 their Councillors were drawn from a wider cross-section of the community than the Moderates, but the most influential member of the Group nevertheless represented the older business links. William Martin was a chartered accountant who had been a business associate of Sir Myers Wayman. He had many commercial interests including the Silver Grid fish and chip shops which had branches throughout the town and the Martin Group of 15 garages and four caravan sales sites which were sold for £9 million in 1977.

Martin had served on Sunderland Council in the 1930s and 1940s. He returned as an Alderman at the time of the Conservative victory in 1967 and was elected chairman of the Finance Committee. He felt that the Sunderland rates had gone too high and that it was his job to keep them down.

His control of the budgets each municipal year was greater than that of the Conservative leaders, of whom there were four during their five years of control.

The Labour Movement

The Labour Party has controlled Sunderland Council continuously since 1945 apart from a brief break from 1967 to 1972. It has also held all the parliamentary seats, with the exception of Sunderland South between 1952 and 1964. The shape of 21st-century Sunderland owes much to Labour politicians.

The first Labour Councillor was elected to Sunderland Town Council in 1891. A year later he was joined by Thomas Summerbell, who became the most important Labour figure at the turn of the century. Summerbell was closely involved with the Council takeover and expansion of the tramway system before becoming the town's first Labour MP from 1906–10.

Labour achieved only limited success between the wars. It controlled Sunderland Council for three years from 1935, with Summerbell's son becoming Mayor, and only held both Sunderland seats during 1929–31. The post-war contrast could not have been more striking.

The Labour Party structure in Sunderland in the second part of the 20th century was quite complex. The District Party was a committee with delegates from the Constituency Labour Parties of Sunderland South and Sunderland North which were established in 1950. Prior to this all Sunderland voters had elected two MPs. From the 1970s Houghton and Washington Constituency also sent representatives to the District Party, which was later renamed the Local Government Committee.

A fifth Labour organisation was the Council's Labour Group. Sometimes different factions of the party controlled different elements. In the early 1980s the Left controlled the District and Sunderland South and North Constituency organisations, but not the Houghton and Washington Constituency or the Council Labour Group.

The Sunderland Labour party had grown out of the Labour Representation Association, the Independent Labour Party and the Sunderland Trades Council which represented the unions. The trade unions continued to play a significant role in the Labour Party, both in providing finance and also having a stranglehold in choosing council and parliamentary candidates, but this influence declined markedly at the end of the 20th century.

There was strong support for trade unionism among many working-class people on Wearside. This was particularly the case in industries such as coalmining, which had a record of poor industrial relations and where the Durham Miners Association, which became part of the National Union of Mineworkers, was seen as crucial in defending miners' rights. Unions

were also significant in shipbuilding, where workers could be laid off with
little notice. Several trade union leaders, such as David Hopper, the
General Secretary of the Durham Area of the National Union of
Mineworkers, came from Sunderland.

Politically the most important trade union element in the town was the
Wearmouth Lodge of the National Union of Mineworkers. The NUM
influence became even more significant after Sunderland's boundaries were
extended in 1967 and 1974 to take in former mining areas. The influence
of the workers in the shipyards, such as the Boilermakers, was less because
they were split among different unions, although there was the co-
ordinating Wear Confederation of Shipbuilders and Engineers. The
shipuilders' influence was not on the scale of the miners. Mining councillors were able to delay moves to introduce smokeless zones in the town
because of the fear of losing jobs in the pits.

The number of trade union officials who represented Labour on the
Town Council also reflected the fact that councillors did not receive
attendance allowances until 1974. There would have been real financial
hardship for many working men in becoming Councillors. Trade union
officials had, however, almost completely disappeared from the Labour
Council membership by the end of the 20th century. This reflected decline
of the influence, and indeed the interest, of the unions in the Labour Party.

The Sunderland and District Trades Council, established in 1884, was
an umbrella organisation for unions with links to the national Trades
Union Council. The different branches of the local unions could affiliate to
the Trades Council and although many representatives were Labour Party
members, not all were. Communist and Conservative supporters were
representatives at various times. Nevertheless the Trades Council was often
a useful training ground for aspiring Labour politicians.

The Labour Party always had a significant number of middle-class
members. Some of its earliest councillors had
to set up their own businesses as many
employers blacklisted them because of their
political activities. By the 1960s there were
also more professional people joining the
party.

The Labour Leaders of the Council in the
second half of the 20th century reflected
different strands in the party. Sir Jack Cohen
was a draper, Charles Slater a solicitor, Len

A rally organised by the
Sunderland Trades Council in
Burdon Road in the early
1980s. Bob Clay, the future MP
for Sunderland North, is
carrying the Passenger
Transport Executive Shop
Stewards Committee's banner.

Harper a teacher, Eric Bramfitt and Bryn Sidaway former colliery electricians, Colin Anderson a civil servant and Bob Symonds also a colliery electrician then personnel officer.

The leaders without close union links needed to have the support of powerful trade unionist Councillors. In the case of Cohen in the 1950s and 1960s this was provided by Joseph Hoy, the most influential Labour councillor of his day. Hoy was a miner who came from a family with strong trade union and Methodist traditions. Nonconformist Church background was a feature of several of the members of the Labour Party. He also had links with another organisation linked to the Labour movement – the Workers Education Association – as he studied economics and history before beginning his trade union and political career.

Joseph Hoy and many other Labour Councillors were also magistrates, as were several businessmen and industrialists in the 1940s and 1950s.

Labour councillors have always taken decisions on policy and tactics at

Sir Jack Cohen (1897–1982) and Lady Kitty Cohen. Sir Jack, a draper, was a member of Sunderland Council for 41 years from 1929 and leader of the Labour Group in the 1950s and 1960s; he was Mayor from 1949 to 1950. Lady Cohen was also a member of the Council and Mayor from 1961 to 1962. He was chairman of the Health Committee from 1945 to 1967 and of the Sunderland Area Hospital Management Committee from 1948 to 1970. Sir Jack was knighted in 1965 in recognition of his contribution to health issues.

Joseph Hoy (1899–1976) was a miner who served as Secretary of the Sunderland General Strike Committee and as chairman of the Wearmouth Miners' Lodge. He was a leading Councillor and Alderman from 1931 to 1970 and Mayor from 1957 to 1958. He had a long involvement with policing, being chairman of the Sunderland Watch Committee and the National Police Council for many years. Hoy was also a member of the Northern Gas Board and Chairman of the Northern Gas Users Consultative Committee.

Len Harper (1928–1983), a headmaster, was a Labour Councillor for Southwick from 1957 until he was defeated by the Liberals 25 years later. Harper, who had a special interest in theatre and the arts, was Leader of the Council from 1976 to 1979 and Mayor from 1979 to 1981.

the group meeting before Council meetings. Inevitably there have often been less formal caucus meetings of like-minded councillors before the group and indeed, at times, pre-caucus meetings of smaller numbers!

The long period of Labour control has meant that the most significant obstacles to the leadership have come mainly from within the party rather than the small opposition parties. The Council Labour Group has often not been as monolithic as it has appeared, with different factions pressing their own agendas and personality clashes, but this has usually taken place out of the public eye.

The central control of the Council leadership has certainly weakened from the days of Jack Cohen and Charles Slater, who ruled the Labour Group with a rod of iron. A greater degree of democracy has, however, been accompanied by more political instability, with four Labour leaders in the 12 years from 1990 as opposed to the three in the previous 36 years. The abolition of committees in 2000, following government legislation, has also meant greater competition for the few cabinet positions and changes in those elected by the group.

In parliamentary politics surprisingly few of Sunderland's Labour MPs, both from the South and North constituencies and those that covered the area added in 1974, have achieved national prominence. Fred Willey was Secretary of State for Land and Natural Resources in the 1964 government while Joyce Quinn held various posts in the 1997 government and Chris Mullin has also served twice as a minister. There has certainly been a tendency to select candidates with local connections rather than those with wider reputations, reflecting the slightly insular nature of Sunderland politics. Similarly local council parties have tended to select members who live in their wards.

The Liberals, Independents and Other Parties

The significance of the Liberals in Sunderland has been much reduced since World War One. In the 1950s and 1960s the Liberals were a dormant force in Sunderland politics. After 1952 the party did not fight any parliamentary elections until 1974. It was also in the 1970s that the Liberals were again represented on the Council.

The Liberals' highpoint came in 1982 when the Liberal/Social Democrat

Alliance had eight Councillors, reflecting the national prominence of the Alliance. This total subsequently declined to the three seats in Thornholme Ward, and the Liberals have failed to replace the Conservatives as the main opposition party as they did in several of the neighbouring local authorities.

There were a number of Independent Councillors for different

wards over the years. The St Chads (East Herrington) Councillors who came in from the Rural District in 1967 were Independents, but voted with the Conservatives. Most others were Labour supporters, including several who had been deselected by their ward parties.

The Communist party contested the 1945 General Election in Sunderland as well as some seats in

Richard Ewart and Fred Willey (left and right centre), the Labour candidates for Sunderland in 1945, are seen here, wearing rosettes, after depositing their nominations with the Mayor. Richard Ewart died while still an MP in 1952. Fred Willey had a long and distinguished career as an MP, Cabinet Minister and chairman of the Parliamentary Labour Party before retiring in 1983. He was effective in lobbying for Sunderland's interests at national level.

'Flacker' Norman was a Colliery Overman who was an Independent Socialist member of the Borough Council for Silksworth from 1968 to 1971 and again from 1975 to 1986 and also of the County Council from 1977 to 1986. He won the seat by standing against the official Labour candidates, although he was ultimately defeated by them. In a community such as the mining village of Silksworth it was possible for a local personality to defeat the party machine.

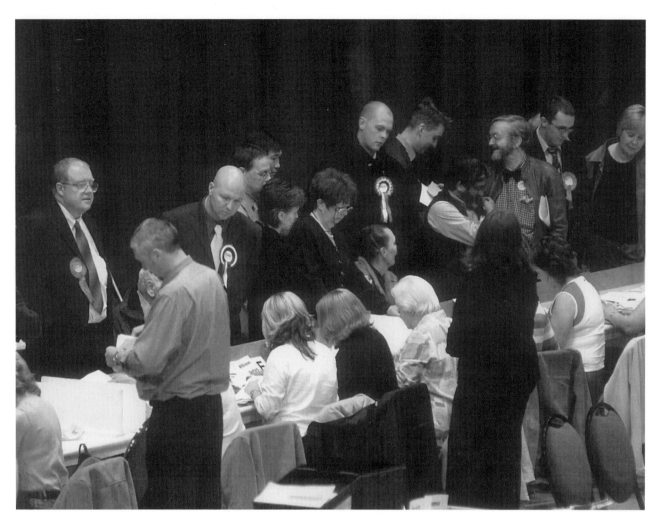

Candidates from the Labour, Liberal and British National parties observe the count at the Council elections in 2003. Sunderland has become well-known for its rapidity in counting votes, particularly in parliamentary elections.

local authority wards. They were always unsuccessful although Tom Richardson, their 1945 parliamentary candidate, became a member of Houghton Urban District Council. The Communists were also active in the trade unions and on the Trades Council.

In the early 2000s the British National Party made a concerted effort to gain seats on Sunderland Council. In 2003, when they attempted to capitalise on media scare stories and rumours about immigration, they came second in a number of seats. They also benefited from being seen as a vehicle for a protest vote against the Labour administration.

CHAPTER 6

Sunderland Life

This chapter looks at the life of people in Sunderland beyond the walls of the shipyards, factories, shops, offices and schools. It covers subjects such as the health of the population and how they spent their spare time.

Health and Hospitals

Throughout the second half of the 20th century Sunderland had a poorer health record than the national average, with pockets of bad health being concentrated in certain parts of the town. The drive to improve health influenced several areas of Council policy. It was an important factor in slum clearance and the building of the Council estates.

The report of the County Borough's Medical Officer of Health for 1948, the year that the National Health Service (NHS) was established, gives an insight into the health of Sunderland in the 1940s. The figure included:

	Sunderland	England and Wales
Birth Rate:	21.4%	17.9%
Death Rate:	12.4%	10.8%

213 children died under the age of one, producing an infant mortality

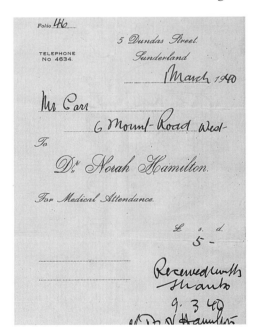

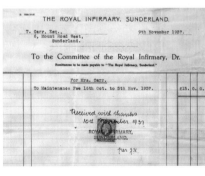

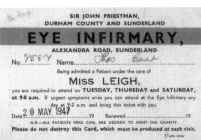

The bills from the Royal Infirmary and Dr Norah Hamilton and the request from the Eye Infirmary that 'All patients that can are desired to assist the Charity' are a reminder that before the National Health Service it was normal to pay for health care.

Monkwearmouth and Southwick Hospital in Newcastle Road, Fulwell, opened in 1932 to replace the former building in Roker Avenue. Both it and the new Eye Infirmary were built with the assistance of the Government's Commissioner for Special Areas. In the 1940s the Council ran the town's hospitals, with the exception of the Royal and Eye Infirmaries. In 1950 Monkwearmouth became the Orthopaedic and Accident Hospital because it was nearest to heavy industry, where many of the accident cases came from.

rate of 55 per 1,000 live births, significantly higher than the national average of 34 per 1,000 live births. The death rate for children in Sunderland born outside marriage (163 as opposed to 3,710 legitimate births) was far higher at 80 per 1,000 illegitimate births. During 1948 2,250 people died in Sunderland. Of these 711 deaths were due to heart diseases, 368 to cancer, 320 to respiratory diseases and 132 to tuberculosis. The report felt that the most serious problem confronting preventive medicine was the infection of children at home from tuberculosis. 29 out of the 2,098 cases of tuberculosis notified in 1948 were children. Other infectious diseases notified included 2,269 cases of measles and 407 of scarlet fever, but the cases of diphtheria had fallen to 34.

The responsibility for hospital provision for all these illnesses passed in July 1948 to the Sunderland Area Hospitals Management Committee, whose territory extended south to Horden and west to Houghton-le-Spring. It undertook responsibility for more than 20 hospitals which had previously been administered by voluntary bodies (as in the case of the Royal Infirmary) or by the local authority (the Municipal, later the General Hospital). All but the General, the Infirmary and Ryhope General, a

The Chester Wing of Sunderland Royal Hospital – the fourth name of the Municipal then General then District Hospital. During the late 1990s and early 2000s several new buildings were put up on this site.

wartime 'hutment' hospital, were specialist hospitals. Several dealt with patients who suffered from diseases highlighted in the Medical Officer's report. Grindon Hall, Boldon and Seaham Hall Sanatoriums and Havelock Hospital, for instance, dealt with tuberculosis, but many cases still had to be treated outside the area. Cherry Knowle Hospital, which catered for psychiatric patients, was separately managed.

The Sunderland Area Hospitals Management Committee started closing the smaller hospitals soon after it was formed. In addition, as tuberculosis was eradicated and infectious diseases declined, their specialist hospitals were converted to other uses and later closed. By 1966 the number of hospitals had been almost halved. In 1978 the Sunderland District Hospital was created by the amalgamation of the General and Maternity Hospitals and the construction of an £11 million new building including accident facilities. Further new building on the District site led to the closure of the Royal Infirmary in 1995.

The number of hospital beds also declined as more people were treated as out-patients or remained in hospitals for less time after operations. Other provision was made in the 1990s by the St Benedict's Hospice opened at Monkwearmouth Hospital and the private hospital built by BUPA in Washington.

The National Assistance Act of 1948 placed responsibility for providing residential accommodation for elderly people, as well as services for people with disabilities, with local authorities. Sunderland Council established 21 residential homes. From the 1980s care for the elderly was increasingly provided in private nursing homes. In 2002 there were about 40 private residential homes in the city, as opposed to six provided by the Council.

When the NHS was set up in 1948 it took over responsibility for the medical and dental services as well as hospitals. The Council's Medical Officer of Health retained responsibility for investigating infectious disease, antenatal and post-natal and child welfare clinics. Several of these municipal responsibilities passed to the NHS at local government reorganisation in 1974.

Under the NHS doctors continued to practise in their existing surgeries, but now provided a free service for their patients. From the 1950s they increasingly began to work in partnerships and tended to be based in health centres or purpose-built practice buildings with treatment rooms and specialist nursing support.

The dental service likewise became free in 1948, although some charges were later introduced. By the beginning of the 21st century many dental practices were for, or also catered for, private patients. There were nevertheless still more NHS dentists on Wearside than in many other parts of the country.

In 2003 the Sunderland Teaching Primary Care Trust, which replaced the Sunderland Health Authority in 2002, is responsible for the delivery of patient care through general practitioners and nurses at local surgeries, dentists and opticians and for commissioning care from the two local Hospital Trusts. These are the City Hospitals Sunderland NHS Trust, which provides care in the Sunderland Royal (formerly the District) Hospital, the Sunderland Eye Infirmary and, to a limited extent, in Ryhope General Hospital. The South of Tyne and Wearside Mental Health NHS Trust administer Cherry Knowle, where the Victorian building is about to be replaced by new facilities, and Monkwearmouth Hospitals. In 2003 the City Hospital Trust was awarded the top three star rating for its performance and the other two Trusts gained two stars.

Health and hospital services have vastly improved in the 55 years after the formation of the National Health Service. This shows in the infant mortality rate falling to 7.5 per 1,000 live births in 1998 from 55 in 1948. The general health of Sunderland people is, nevertheless, still poorer than the national average. The number of people who stated

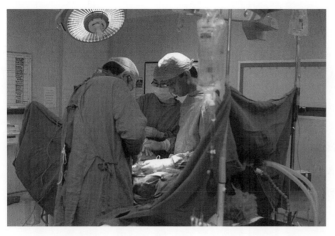

An operation being carried out at Sunderland Royal Hospital. In 2003 Sunderland was one of only 13 hospital trusts in the country which had been awarded three star status for three years running.

that they had a long term illness or disability in the 2001 census was 24.1 percent, as opposed to 18.2 percent for England and Wales.

The Sunderland Health Authority's *Health Improvement for the Sunderland Area 1999–2002* report gave the life expectancy rates for people in the city compared with the national average:

	Sunderland	England and Wales
Men	72.1 years	74.1 years
Women	77.4 years	79.5 years

This was the third shortest life expectancy for women in England. The main causes of death in Sunderland were cancer (27 percent) and heart disease (22 percent). These were the same two main causes as in 1948, although cancer had now overtaken heart disease as the major killer. The third major cause of death was stroke; in 1948 it was respiratory disease, reflecting the heavy industries many worked in. The rise in the significance of cancer and stroke deaths reflected the fact that people were living longer.

As in 1948 there were health blackspots in certain areas of the town, with a good level of health in the middle-class areas. The *Health Improvement* report mentioned that the state of health in Sunderland reflected 'the legacy of long-term unemployment, the previous heavy industry (coalmining and shipbuilding) and its subsequent decline, poor housing conditions and an unhealthy lifestyle, which have left a legacy and continue to be associated with a health record which is worse than the rest of the country. These health problems are reflected in both physical and mental health problems.'

Lifestyle was also identified as a major determinant of health in the report, which stated that Sunderland people had a high prevalence of lifestyles, such as high smoking levels, low rates of exercise and unhealthy diet, which led to the development of cancer and heart disease. At the beginning of the 21st century encouraging healthier lifestyles, through measures such as health education and encouraging people to take exercise and stop smoking, is a priority not only for the National Health Service, but also for the City Council in Sunderland.

Religion

The history of places of worship in Sunderland since 1945 has been generally one of a decline in numbers, little different from the nationwide pattern of fewer members and fewer clergy. There have, however, been exceptions to this, notably in the case of Evangelical and Pentecostal Christian churches and the places of worship for the Asian community.

The Sunday School Good Friday service outside the Town Hall in 1957. Three columns of thousands of members of the Sunday Schools, each behind their own banners, marched behind Salvation Army bands and the whole of Fawcett Street was crammed full for the service. The event still takes place, on a much reduced scale, outside the Civic Centre.

One major problem for churches was that their places of worship tended to be centred in areas already built up by the end of the 19th century, whose populations declined as the inhabitants moved out to the new estates on the outskirts. In the East End St John's and Holy Trinity Churches of England and St Patrick's Roman Catholic Church closed along with the Methodist and Presbyterian churches and missions. Several new churches were built in the housing estates, but it is probably true to say that the churches that have prospered have been those in the middle-class areas.

To cope with a declining number of clergy the Bishop of Durham's Commission on Sunderland recommended in 1970 that the Church of England parishes in the Wearmouth Deanery should become one team ministry with six or seven pastoral units or clusters. There was opposition to the proposal and it foundered after the death of Ian Ramsey, the much-respected Bishop of Durham, in 1972. Twenty years later the Church of England began to introduce team ministries for certain areas of the city and team ministries serving several churches have also been implemented by other denominations.

There has been only limited union between the different Christian denominations, the most significant being the formation of the United Reformed Church from the Congregational and Presbyterian Churches in 1972. On the other hand more ecumenical co-operation has developed via organisations such as City Centre Churches Together through joint services and pulpit exchanges. The most obvious sign of churches working together has been the ecumenical Oxclose Church in Washington, opened in the late 1970s. Here all the congregations of the Anglican, Methodist and United Reformed Church worship together.

Outside the traditional Christian denominations, the independent Evangelical and Christian denominations have fared better. One of the most prominent, the Bethesda Free Church, dated back to 1844 and three missions were established in the suburbs in the post-war years. The Sunderland Free Church in Stockton Road, built in 1978, was a secession from Bethesda. Other well-supported Evangelical churches in the early 2000s include Bethany Church in Houghton and Hope Church in the East End.

The Jewish congregations have fallen markedly since 1945 as the children of members moved away from the town for higher education and work; they often settled in areas with bigger Jewish communities. In the

The cover of this brochure marked another important Good Friday event on Wearside. It marked the centennial Good Friday Concert at Hetton-le-Hole Methodist Church in 1970. The Church is in the centre and names around the edge are oratorios that had been performed over the previous 100 years. The colliery scenes at the bottom of the cover are a reminder of the strong links between Methodism and pit workers in many mining villages.

Jim Taylor, Vicar of St Mark's in Millfield, speaking to members of his congregation after a service in 1970. Taylor was joint chairman of the Millfield Residents Association which opposed the widespread demolition of housing in the area. He was one of a number of clergy who developed a rapport with their parishioners. Another was Canon Gordon Hopkins, Vicar of Pallion from 1939 to 1970.

Crowds queue to enter the new Fulwell Methodist Church in 1961. Designed by the Sunderland architect Stanley Milburn, the church was on the first floor with ancillary rooms below, a revival of an old Methodist practice. The spire was later demolished.

2001 census only 114 people were recorded as being of the Jewish religion. This decline has led to the closure of one of the city's synagogues along with other Jewish institutions such as the Joel Intract residential home for the elderly.

The number of people following religions other than Christianity, although small, increased during the second half of the 20th century, especially following immigration from Asia. The 2001 census recorded 261 from the Hindu faith, 272 Buddhists, 547 Sikhs and 2,099 Muslims. The Muslims worshipped in an adapted terrace house in Chester Road, while in the 1990s the Sikhs acquired the former Anglican Christ Church hall for their Gurduwara Temple; the church buildings became Ashbrooke Hall, used not only by the Sikhs, but also by the wider community.

The change of religious use of Christ Church and the nearby Park Road Methodist Church, which became the Pentecostal Metro Church International in 2003, were a reminder that although the balance between religions and between the Christian denominations was changing, many Sunderland people still attended worship. While a majority might no longer do so, no less that 228,815 still recorded themselves as Christian in the 2001 census.

Leisure

Many publications have been produced on different aspects of leisure in the city, ranging from those covering pubs, cinemas and museums to the many books on Sunderland Association Football Club. The following section is a broad survey of some of Sunderland's leisure activities, highlighting a few topics.

The wide range of books on the football club reflects its importance in the life of Wearside. In the years since World War Two local people have increasingly seen the club as a significant expression of the city's identity and its mixed fortunes have attracted more attention in the national media than any other part of life in Sunderland.

The popularity of the club in the immediate post-war years after Football League games began again in 1946 can be seen from the record attendance of 1,000,483 spectators at the matches at Roker Park during 1949–50. Of these 68,004 watched the match against Newcastle in March 1950.

In 1946 Sunderland AFC hoped to regain its pre-war success when it was one of the country's leading clubs. Its fortunes were, however, to be much more mixed, with relegation to the Second Division in 1958; at that time Sunderland had been in the First Division longer than any other club. This followed a crisis in the club when it was fined and the chairman William Ditchburn, four directors, including William Martin, and five players were suspended by the Football Association who found that illegal payments had been made to players. The High Court later rescinded the punishments, but the affair undoubtedly damaged Sunderland AFC.

Sunderland AFC was promoted in 1964 and relegated again in 1970. It was while in the Second Division in 1973 that Sunderland won the FA Cup for the second time, beating the mighty Leeds 1-0. Promotion and relegation followed again several times in the 10 years from 1977.

Ian Porterfield scoring Sunderland's winning goal in the 1-0 victory over Leeds in the FA Cup Final at Wembley on 5 May 1973. This has been the high point of the football club's mixed fortunes in the years since World War Two.

The programme produced for the football club's last League match at Roker Park on 3 May 1997. The following season the club moved to the Stadium of Light.

In 1987 the club was relegated for the first time to the Third Division, but returned a year later to the Second with the club moving between the top two divisions (from 1992 the Premier League and the new First Division) during the next 15 years, being champions of the latter in 1996 and 1999. In 2003 Sunderland were once again relegated and have yet to break out of the yo-yo pattern of promotion and relegation experienced since 1958.

By the 1990s it was clear that Sunderland AFC would need to move from Roker Park, which had been its home since 1898. The club first wanted to relocate to a new site close to Nissan, but instead it was decided that the new all-seater stadium should be built on the site of Wearmouth

Colliery. The impressive Stadium of Light, opened in 1997, is one of the largest in the country.

In 1945 the other major centre for sporting activity besides Roker Park was Ashbrooke, which had developed as the centre for amateur sport, notably cricket, rugby, athletics, tennis, hockey and bowls. Ashbrooke was also the venue for various sporting championships as well as playing host to international touring teams in the post-war years.

Ashbrooke's role as a major provider for amateur sport became less important after the local authority developed sports centres from the 1970s. Crowtree Leisure Centre was one of the country's largest indoor sports and recreation centres. Other Council sports centres were provided at Hetton, Houghton, Washington and Hendon. The Silksworth Sports and Recreation Centre, developed from 1981 on the former colliery site, included a dry ski-slope and a large indoor tennis centre. In addition to the major sports centres there were of course many local sports organisations including football, cricket, cycling and bowls clubs, often with their own grounds.

For many Sunderland people in the years following World War Two a trip by tram to Roker or Seaburn was a popular way to spend a day, especially for families with children who could paddle or swim in the sea. As more

The swimming pool at the Raich Carter Sports Centre in Hendon, opened in 2001. The centre, named after the captain of the 1937 FA Cup winning team, also includes a sports hall and gymnasium.

A group of Sunderland Clarion Cycling Club members on a run in 1948. In the 1940s cycling clubs thrived, especially with the restrictions on motoring. Many clubs also organised social events; the Sunderland Clarion had a clubhouse in Millfield.

The Seaburn Hall was built in 1938 to provide a concert, dance and conference hall as well as a restaurant for visitors to the town's seaside. In the 1960s it was serving 100,000 meals a year. It was later replaced by the Seaburn Leisure Centre.

families had cars in which they could travel further afield or took holidays abroad, the beaches became less popular and most of the attractions, apart from the funfair, disappeared. Since 1988, however, one weekend each year when the seafront is as popular as ever is that of the Sunderland International Airshow, which attracts over a million spectators.

The Council had provided a museum and library service since the mid-19th century. In 1879 the Library and Museum in Borough Road was opened. The building was supplemented by branch libraries from the 1900s, but was very overcrowded by the 1930s. It was only in 1964, however, that the much-needed extension was completed. A number of new branch libraries were developed from the 1950s to serve the new estates and several more libraries were added after Sunderland's boundaries were extended in 1967 and 1974, with the major new Washington Town Centre Library being opened in 1976. The museums, run after 1974 by Tyne and Wear Museums, also expanded outside their main site, notably with Monkwearmouth Station Museum in 1973.

Major expansion of the city's cultural facilities began in 1995 when a new, larger City Library was opened in the former Binns building in Fawcett Street; it also housed the Northern Gallery for Contemporary Art which had previously been an independent arts centre in Stockton Road. In 2003 the City Library is the centre for a service which includes 20 other libraries, some combined with electronic village halls, two mobile libraries, an information technology mobile library and a schools library service. This list shows that the public libraries are providing services beyond the loan of books, particularly in the provision of information and of computer and internet access.

The Children's Library in 1966. This was one of the expanded facilities in the Central Library, Museum and Art Gallery opened two years previously.

Important developments also took place in Sunderland's museums, with an education service being developed from the 1980s and a new generation of displays with interactive exhibits and audiovisual programmes from the 1990s. The Borough Road building closed in 1999 for a major rebuilding programme which included a new entrance, several new galleries and visitor facilities and the construction of the new Winter Gardens; many Sunderland people still fondly recalled the original Winter Gardens destroyed during the war. Sunderland Museum and Winter Gardens reopened in 2001 and quickly became one of the most popular visitor attractions in the region. The museums in Sunderland, like the libraries and the Tourist Information Centre, won several national awards in the late 1990s/early 2000s.

Crowds queue outside the entrance to the Museum and Winter Gardens on 21 July 2001, the day the Museum reopened to the public after complete refurbishment and the construction of the new Winter Gardens.

Ralph Baxter, a Labour Councillor, was closely involved with cultural developments in Sunderland and the wider region from 1974 to 2002. The posts he held included chairman of the Leisure Committee and the Empire Theatre Trust, vice-chairman of the Tyne and Wear Museums Committee and chairman of the North of England Museums Service.

The National Glass Centre, a Tyne and Wear Development Corporation project, opened in 1998 in a striking building on the riverside whose facilities included areas for glassmaking demonstrations and exhibitions of contemporary glass. It lay adjacent to the St Peter's Riverside Sculpture Trail, part of Sunderland's public art programme.

The Empire Theatre has been a major centre for entertainment in Sunderland since its opening in 1907. It remained a popular venue for variety acts, attracting stars such Laurel and Hardy, in the 1940s and early 1950s. There was also the Empire Christmas pantomime, which became a Sunderland institution. After the development of television, audiences began to drop off and the Theatre closed in 1959. It was, however, acquired and reopened by the Council using compensation they had been awarded for a replacement for the Victoria Hall destroyed during World War Two; this had been used for public events such as concerts.

The Council subsidies allowed the Empire, which now had a Civic Theatre subtitle, to develop a wider programme. In 1966 the Empire, which had recently increased its annual audience from 150,000 to 250,000, saw its role as 'theatre as a social service' which would encourage young people to appreciate its art as well as providing entertainment for adults. It was now attracting the Sadler's Wells Opera, the Royal Ballet, the Royal Shakespeare and similar companies as well as jazz and pop stars.

As the biggest theatre between Leeds and Edinburgh, with a large stage particularly suitable for opera and ballet, the Empire has been able to pull in some of the major touring productions; in 2003 SFX, the private firm who had managed the Theatre since 2000, announced plans to enlarge the

The Empire Theatre, designed by W. and T.R. Milburn and opened by Vesta Tilley in 1907, is one of the region's two major theatres. Its purchase by the Corporation was a far-sighted move and it continues to thrive, although now under private management.

The Beatles at the Empire in February 1963, the first of their two appearances at the Theatre that year. Their records were already topping the charts and they would go on to be international legends.

facilities to take major West End shows. While some of the major companies have, however, preferred to go to the Theatre Royal in Newcastle, the Empire has been able to attract an audience from throughout the North East for popular productions.

It is ironic that the Empire has outlasted all the cinemas in Sunderland, which at one time threatened to vanquish theatres completely. In the years immediately after World War Two when cinemas were attracting peak audiences there were around 15 cinemas in Sunderland. With the increasing number of television sets from 1953 onwards the cinemas began to close, often being converted into bingo halls. In 1999 the Canon (formerly the Ritz and then the ABC) closed and Sunderland became probably the largest centre of population without a cinema. Several plans for multi-screen cinemas were put forward, but it was only in 2003 that work began on building a new 12-screen multiplex cinema which is part of a new leisure development in High Street West.

In addition to the Empire and cinemas there were many other places for

The New Rink was one of the most popular social venues for young people in the 1940s, 1950s and 1960s. It was also one of the largest dance halls in the country. It was owned by George and Alfred Black and shared a common entrance with their Ritz cinema in Holmeside. In the 1940s and 1950s no alcohol was allowed apart from at special events such as the press ball.

Bobby Thompson (1911–1988), 'Wor Bobby' or 'The Little Waster', with a record compiled from his comedy turns which was a big local success in the 1970s. He was one of Wearside's most popular entertainers in pubs and clubs. His career peaked with BBC Radio's *Wot Cheor Geordie* and he topped the bill at the Empire in pantomime. A television series was a failure and he returned to performing in local clubs.

Amy Emms (1904–1998) was a leading figure in Durham quilting who helped to ensure the craft's survival into the 21st century. She taught classes at the East End Community centre from 1951 to 1967 and her work has inspired groups such as the Sunderland Museum Quilters who still practise the craft today. When she died the *Guardian* described her as 'one of the last true folk artists in Britain'.

evening entertainment in Sunderland. Dance halls, particularly the Rink and Seaburn Hall, night clubs, bingo halls and bowling alleys have all played their part in providing leisure for Sunderland people. Social clubs have been a particularly strong feature of North East life. They often served the areas they were situated in, but others catered for those working in particular industries. The clubs were particularly strong in the 1960s and 1970s. In 1972 there were 72 clubs in Sunderland registered with the Club and Institute Union. The clubs often presented major comic acts as entertainment.

Public houses were, of course, where many Wearsiders enjoyed some of their leisure hours. In 1945 there was a wide range of licensed premises ranging from the basic Victorian pubs of the East End to the grand Edwardian buildings, such as the Dun Cow and the Mountain Daisy. Many of the pubs were modernised in the 1960s and 1970s, only to be refitted later in a neo-Victorian style. During the 1990s a number of larger licensed premises, which also served food, were opened in the city centre, to be followed by numerous wine bars.

Pubs and clubs were one way in which Sunderland people could spend their leisure time. Another was by taking part in the various societies which existed in the city. They ranged widely from the supporters of various charitable groups to photographic, musical and gardening societies. Some, such as the Antiquarian Society of 1900 were long established, while others

The Station Hotel, one of Sunderland's less elaborate pubs, in 1965, shortly before it was closed. Beyond St John's Church and School is the Welcome Tavern of 1915 which still survives today, unlike the other buildings. The station after which the pub was named had closed over a century before. The trend for renaming pubs lay several years ahead!

The Mountain Daisy in Hylton Road, one of Sunderland's finest Edwardian public houses. It has an extremely fine back room with the walls and the front of the bar composed of glazed tiles. There were several public rooms on the first floor including a billiard saloon.

such as the local history groups covering specific parts of the town developed in the 1980s and 1990s. A few groups acquired their own premises; the Drama Club developed their own theatre in the former Royalty Church premises and the Model Engineering Society's miniature railway test track has become a feature of Roker Park.

The Media

The 75th anniversary edition of *The Sunderland Echo and Shipping Gazette* published on 22 December 1948. Because of restriction on the use of paper it was only eight pages.

The *Sunderland Echo* remains by far the most important source of local news for the city. At the time of its centenary in December 1973 Fred Willey, MP for Sunderland North, wrote of the evening paper's 'saturation readership'. The style of the *Echo* has changed over the years. In the 1940s the policy was to record news in detail, with topics such as the arrival and departure of ships from the Wear being covered. From the 1960s more emphasis was placed on features and weekly columns, under the names of particular journalists.

The *Echo* built a new printing hall at its Bridge Street premises, but in 1976 it abandoned them when it moved to its new office and production centre at Pennywell close to the A19. This saw the replacement of hot metal linotype machine printing by photo-composition and web-offset printing. Colour photographs now became a feature of the paper. The plant at Pennywell also carries out contract printing work for the northern editions of national papers.

Portsmouth and Sunderland Newspapers, which also published the evening papers in Hartlepool and Portsmouth, was controlled by the descendants of Samuel Storey who had been the principal founder of the *Echo* in 1873. The local group became North East Press in 1991 after the acquisition of the *Shields Gazette*, whose printing was transferred to Pennywell, and weekly papers in Northumberland. Following a division among the Storey family it passed out of their ownership and entered the 21st century under the control of the Johnston Press.

The Conservative politics of the Storeys tended to be reflected in the editorial comments of the *Echo* for many years, although they cannot be said to have influenced the voting trends of the majority of the population of Sunderland. More important were probably the campaigns run by the newspaper which included issues such as poor housing and sewage in the sea and returning the Victoria Hall disaster memorial to Mowbray Park.

The regional morning daily newspapers – the *Journal* printed in Newcastle and, to a lesser extent, the *Northern Echo* in Darlington – have also covered Sunderland to a more limited extent and with far less local

readership. In the 1980s the *Sunderland and Washington Times* free weekly was widely read, but its role was later taken over by the *Sunderland Star* produced by the *Echo*.

Television played an increasingly important role in home entertainment from the 1950s. The BBC's Pontop Pike transmitter opened in May 1953 just in time for Wearsiders to receive good-quality reception of the Coronation. The region's commercial station Tyne Tees Television started broadcasting in 1959. The joint programme directors were George and Alfred Black of Sunderland, who had been partners in their father's cinema chain. Local radio has been provided first in 1968 by BBC's Radio Durham and then by Radio Newcastle and the commercial Metro and Century Radios and by SunFM, the only station based in the city.

The *Echo's* 75th anniversary edition would have been produced using these hot metal plates in the printing hall at the back of the *Echo's* premises in Bridge Street.

The City of Sunderland in 2003

Springwell

Hylton
Red House

Roker

Monkwearmouth

Hylton
Castle

Southwick

Castletown

Nissan
Works

Washington

South
Hylton

Hendon

Blackfell

Pennywell

Town
Centre

Grindon

Plains
Farm

Rickleton

Silksworth

Penshaw

Doxford Park

Doxford
Business
Park

Shiney
Row

Ryhope

A19

Seaham

Houghton-le-Spring

Hetton-le-Hole

East
Rainton

Easington
Lane

-- PASSENGER RAILWAYS
— MAJOR ROADS
▬ CITY BOUNDARY

CHAPTER 7

Sunderland Transformed

The River Wear and the A19

This final section of the book looks at the changes and the similarities between Sunderland in 2003 and the Sunderland of 1945 which was described in Chapter 1. Some of the illustrations compare a location as it is today with the same view as it was 30 or more years ago.

The physical contrast is best seen from the Wearmouth Bridge, which in 1945 was the centre of many of Sunderland's traditional industries which lay on the river banks. In 2003 these have virtually all vanished apart from the shipping facilities on Corporation Quay and in the South Docks.

The view east from the Bridge is now dominated by the Sunderland University buildings on the former North Sands shipyard. Around the bend of the Wear, next to the University campus, lies the National Glass Centre.

St Peter's Church with the University buildings on the right. Until the 1950s this view from the river would have been obscured by the shipyards and Hallgarth Square.

Looking east from Wearmouth Bridge in 2003. On the north (left) bank new flats are under construction around Deuchar's warehouse while the University campus occupies much of the riverside towards the harbour mouth. Student accommodation has been built on the south bank. The cranes at Corporation Quay are one of the few links with Sunderland's maritime past.

Much of the remainder of the banks is now used for housing. On the north bank close to the Bridge new 'Manhattan-style loft apartments' and penthouse suites are being constructed around the former Deuchar's warehouse. The North Dock, now the Sunderland Marina, is the centre of a mixed development of 500 homes. On the south bank student flats have been built at Panns Bank and on Scotia Quay.

The residential use of the river bank is a reversal of the pattern of the first half of the 20th century when most of the surviving housing was cleared from the riverside. This was mainly to allow the development of industry; the disappearance of such industry has seen new housing return from the 1990s.

Looking west from Wearmouth Bridge, the dominant building on the north bank is Sunderland Football Club's Stadium of Light, built on the site of Wearmouth Colliery. On the south bank the site of the Lambton and Hetton staiths and their railway sidings are now the rather uninspiring Festival Park. Beyond is one of the few surviving shipyard buildings in the former Deptford yard. This is now used by Liebherr, who build large cranes for ships and the offshore oil industry.

Also surviving, on the other side of the Queen Alexandra Bridge, is the undercover yard at Pallion. In 2003 Pallion Engineering is carrying out restoration work on a Manx ferry that had been moored for several years in the Wear. Pallion yard and

1958. The *Cornhill* and another of the Wear tugs take the *Errington Court*, which had been built by William Pickersgill for Court Line, down a busy river past ships waiting to be loaded.

2003. The Wear is empty apart from a few small boats. The National Glass Centre has been constructed on the site of North Sands shipyard and in the distance flats surround the North Dock, now the Sunderland Marina.

1970. Wearmouth Colliery and Staiths. By this date the Staiths were only used for pit waste which was tipped out at sea by hoppers. The slipway of the Deptford shipyard is on the left.

the Wear Dock and Engineering ship and offshore platform repair base at the former Greenwell's yard at the South Docks are the last survivors of Sunderland's maritime industries.

On the site of the Austin & Pickersgill shipyard and Hylton Colliery lies Hylton Riverside Business Park, one of the projects of the Tyne and Wear Development Corporation. This was a result of its early decision to concentrate its industrial and commercial initiatives on its land towards the A19 and return the area below the Queen Alexandra Bridge to 'living, learning and leisure'.

The Development Corporation's policy reflected the fact that by the late 1980s the A19 and the roads leading east and west off it were becoming the commercial spine of Sunderland. They replaced the river and the railway systems which had been the major routes which industry concentrated around in the 19th and first half of the 20th century. North of the Wear Nissan lies close to the A19 and its suppliers feeding components to it on the 'just in time' system are nearby. The other major centre of employment, Doxford International Business Park, is situated adjacent to the A19 south of the river.

2003. The Stadium of Light, home of Sunderland Football Club, now stands on the site of Wearmouth Colliery. On the far left Liebherr Cranes occupy the site of Deptford Shipyard.

The City Centre

Like the river banks, the city centre has seen vast changes since the end of World War Two. It is now bordered on three sides by the inner ring road. The area between Fawcett Street and the Minster has been almost completely redeveloped, reflecting the move westwards of the main shopping and commercial area.

The area to the east of Fawcett Street has physically changed far less. Most of the shops, with the notable exception of Jopling's, and the banks and buildings societies, have moved out. However, it still contains the offices of solicitors and other professions, but these are fewer as more work is now carried out in Newcastle and beyond. In the 1940s, for instance, there were still major architectural practices in Sunderland, such as the Milburns, but these had largely disappeared by the end of the 20th century.

The offices of the major companies which had once been grouped around the centre of Sunderland had all vanished by the 2000s. The public utilities which provided services are now part of larger companies, which are often now subsidiaries of multinational organisations. The companies which still have significant offices in the city tend to locate them on the outskirts, mainly at Doxford Park.

The Town Hall was demolished in 1971, but ironically in 2003 Sunderland Council once again occupy a significant part of Fawcett Street. The rather nondescript buildings erected on the site of the Town Hall now house the social services department and the former Binns east building the

City Library and the careers service, while the Sunderland Housing Group is converting part of the Athenaeum building for its offices. The Housing Group is also adapting the upper storey of the building for accommodation, along with the former Post Office and several former buildings in Sunniside, which is reverting to being a primarily residential area as it was in Victorian times.

The section of High Street West between Fawcett Street and Crowtree Road, now pedestrianised, still remains an important shopping street with major chain stores, but most retail activity is concentrated in the undercover Bridges Centre. The Bridges extension in 2000 greatly improved the quality of shopping in Sunderland.

There are several public buildings around the edge of the city centre. The Museum is the oldest of these, but it has been transformed by the developments of 2001 which include the new entrance and the Winter Gardens. The others – the Civic Centre, Crowtree Leisure Centre, the St Mary's Car Park and Park Lane Interchange – were completed in the last 30 years of the 20th century.

From the East End to Washington New Town

The East End and Monkwearmouth, the historic areas of Sunderland outside the city centre, have been largely redeveloped. The surviving Georgian historic buildings of the East End have, or are about to be, restored, but most of the houses that stood in 1945, including the Garths of 1937, have gone. New housing has been built, but the population has fallen greatly and even the St John and St Patrick's Church School of 1972 closed in the 1990s. The identity of the East End has been lost for some Sunderland people who now refer to it as being part of Hendon, its Victorian neighbour, parts of which have also been rebuilt. Monkwearmouth has retained its distinctiveness better. Although very little of its Victorian housing and of its shopping centre remain, it has two of Sunderland's outstanding buildings, St Peter's Church and Monkwearmouth Station Museum.

Beyond Hendon and Monkwearmouth the suburbs that existed before World War Two have seen fewer changes, although many of the local shops have closed. The 1990s and 2000s have seen new housing and nursing homes on sites such as the former laundries in Fulwell and High Barnes and the edges of Ashbrooke Sports Ground.

The housing estates towards the edge of the old County Borough are among the most noticeable changes in Sunderland since 1945. The Council

1970. It seems hard to believe that this group of buildings, which includes a general dealer's shop, at the corner of Coronation Street survived virtually unchanged so long into the 20th century. The upper floors were no longer used for housing in 1970, but at the end of World War Two there were many substandard houses in the area.

2003. Lumley Tower and its adjacent tower blocks are where many East End residents have lived since the late 1960s. In front of the flats is Phoenix Lodge, built in 1785, which is the oldest surviving Freemasons' Hall in the country.

'Dutch Bungalows' in Park Avenue, Seaburn, in 1992. This and similar suburbs of Sunderland which were built in the inter-war years are among the areas which have changed least since 1945.

1949. Seaburn at its busiest in 1949 with the miniature railway and the fairground enjoying excellent patronage.

Opposite page: **2001.** These vast crowds at Seaburn are now the exception and only gather once a year to see the Sunderland Airshow.

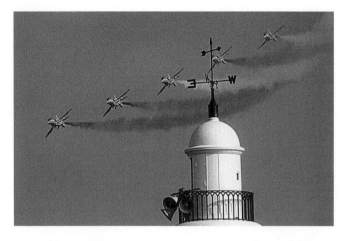

The Red Arrows taking part in the Sunderland Airshow in 2001. They are flying over the 1856 lighthouse which was moved to Roker Cliff Park in 1973.

The Washington F Pit Museum, which consists of the winding house and engine and headstock of the colliery, is one of the few reminders of coal mining on Wearside. The other notable industrial monuments on Wearside include the Bowes Railway, also in Washington, the Ryhope Water Pumping Station and Monkwearmouth Station Museum.

built the majority and most were semi-detached houses, although in the 1960s other types such as the less popular maisonettes were built. Commerce has also encroached on former farmland, most notably at Doxford International Business Park.

The seaside facilities at Roker and Seaburn have declined since the 1960s and they now suffer in comparison with South Shields where there has been more investment in the seafront. They nevertheless still remain an attractive part of Sunderland.

The former pit villages and towns, such as Castletown and Houghton, have of course lost a major source of work with the closure of collieries

and many people have to travel from them to their places of employment. Some work in Washington, where many administrative, commercial and industrial jobs have been created. During the late 1960s, 1970s and 1980s Washington New Town had been the most significant growth point on Wearside for both industry and housing.

Sunderland People

The population of the city of Sunderland measured in the 2001 census was 280,807, a fall of just over 14,000 from a high point in 1981. 22.2 percent were still engaged in manufacturing, but there were now 14.3 percent working in finance/business and 23.3 percent in education, health/social work and other services. The overall unemployment rate of 4.9 percent was significantly higher among men (6.8 percent) than women (2.4 percent). These figures reflect the fact that the call centres and several other new employers rely heavily on a female workforce and in some cases women have become the main wage-earners in the family. This has been a major change in what was very much a male-dominated society.

The collapse of the traditional industries undoubtedly poses problems for male teenagers leaving school who used to go into apprenticeships,

Bartram's South Dock Yard in the late 1940s. This photograph is a reminder that until the 1970s all ships on Wearside were built in the open air and workers had to cope with extremes of weather when carrying out often dangerous tasks, sometimes with material which would be forbidden today. Jobs in the male-orientated heavy industries, such as shipbuilding, are ones which vanished during the second half of the 20th century.

often in industries where their fathers worked, such as shipbuilding. These employment routes disappeared and while Sunderland schoolchildren generally perform well at primary school level, the level of school leavers without qualifications is very high, which means that finding jobs is more difficult.

The people of Sunderland remain a largely indigenous and settled society. 98.1 percent are white and only 2.4 percent were born outside the United Kingdom, one of the lowest levels in the country. The largest non-white ethnic group are the Asian or Asian British (1.0 percent).

Sunderland is still largely a working-class community with low wages and unemployment in certain parts of the city (mainly the Council estates in the former County Borough area) and prosperity in others. In 2003 the average weekly wage in the two Sunderland parliamentary constituencies is £373, while for the Houghton and Washington East constituency it is £414; the North-East average is £399. The stark contrast in the lives of Sunderland people can be seen in comparing the council ward of Thorney Close with Fulwell:

	Unemployed	No Qualifications	Permanently Sick or Disabled
Thorney Close	8.0%	50.3%	14.4%
Fulwell	2.2%	27.3%	5.8%

The areas with high levels of poverty, unemployment and long term ill health are often the areas that suffer from drug-related and other crime.

1930s. The Municipal Hospital and Highfield Institute buildings (formerly the Workhouse) looking south towards Chester Road. They provided free hospital care. The open ground above the buildings had been cultivated for vegetables by the Workhouse residents.

Some of these social problems reflect the lack of aspiration in families in which two generations have experienced long-term unemployment and have low incomes. The challenge of improving health and educational aspects of the lifestyles of some of Sunderland's people is an important one in the 2000s.

The rather depressing figures for some areas might suggest that the problems of the pre-World War Two East End and Monkwearmouth have been transferred to some of the post-1945 estates. It should, however, be stressed that the relative quality of the housing is now far better. Many of the estates are indeed still good places to live in.

National press coverage of the city sometimes tends to concentrate on the negative aspects outlined above – the high level of ill health, low level of educational qualifications and also the fact that it has the lowest Gross Domestic Product of any city in the UK. But other comparisons show that Sunderland is better than the national average in some areas. Out of six notifiable crime headings only two were higher in Sunderland than the England and Wales average.

The middle-class areas of Sunderland, which have lower than the national average figures for unemployment and poor health, have increased during the last half of the 20th century with private housing built on the new estates in areas such as Seaburn Dene, Doxford Park and parts

2002. This view (looking south) of the Sunderland Royal Hospital shows how most of the Victorian workhouse structures have been demolished and replaced by new buildings from the 1970s onwards. The Royal Hospital now provides most of the expanded hospital care on Wearside.

A rag and bone man with his horse-drawn cart in Bainbridge Avenue in 2003. The material he collects today, however, will probably be electrical goods and furniture.

of Washington. Some of the people living in these areas, particularly Washington, work on Tyneside. Conversely others who come to work in Sunderland choose to live in Durham or Newcastle instead and this is undoubtedly a disadvantage when they are decision-makers in the city. As in 1945, many people working in Sunderland also live in Cleadon and Whitburn, which are still outside the municipal boundaries.

The middle-class population has been less static than the majority of the city's people. The children of middle-class parents are more likely to obtain qualifications and move to jobs outside the area. The decline of the Jewish community is a good illustration of this. There has also been less incentive for workers in the traditional industries to move away as coalmining and other similar employment has declined nationwide, and not just in Wearside.

Sunderland has a small middle class, but it is one whose members continue to play an active part in the life of the community in areas such as local churches which are now more likely to be situated in middle-class areas and in societies and organisations like the Ashbrooke Sports Club. Since the disappearance of Bede as a grammar school they have been more likely to send their children to private schools such as Sunderland High or to St Aidan's and St Anthony's. These latter schools attract a significant number of non-Catholics, partly because with sixth forms they are believed to maintain something of the ethos of grammar schools as well as because they are single-sex institutions.

2003. Telegrams have disappeared into history and mobile phones and Email have become common forms of communication on Wearside. This brochure advertising both services was produced by T Mobile, which has one of its customer services offices at Doxford Technology Park.

1950. Sunderland Telegram boys. At this date many Sunderland houses would not have had phones and telegrams were used for urgent messages as well as for greetings for special occasions. They were also used by businesses who had their own short telegraphic addresses such as 'Exporter Sunderland' for the Rose Line.

1951. Hand turning colliery lamp brushes at Cottam Brothers works in Monkwearmouth. **2003.** Producing brooms on a fully automatic machine. Cottams are one of the few Sunderland manufacturing firms of the 1940s who are still in business today. They are almost certainly the oldest family-controlled firm in Sunderland and can trace their origins back to 1858. Their range now includes brushes for cleaning and measuring wear in under-sea gas and oil pipelines.

There is still the common bond among all Wearsiders of pride in coming from Sunderland, but the decline of the traditional industries has contributed to a decline in Wearsiders' confidence. There can be no doubt that the loss of shipbuilding and the other traditional industries has proved a psychological blow to the people of Sunderland who feel part of the city's identity has been taken away. The success of car manufacturing and call centres does not seem to be any replacement for 'the largest shipbuilding town in the world'.

The industrial change appears to have also increased the feeling that the city is faring worse than Newcastle, a claim that frequently appears in the *Sunderland Echo's* letters page in the 2000s. The facts show otherwise. In 2003 the government's 'league tables' place Sunderland above Newcastle in local government and hospitals. Sunderland also has lower rates of council tax and unemployment than its Tyneside neighbour. It is nevertheless true that Sunderland undoubtedly continues to suffer because Newcastle has a far higher public profile, particularly in the national media.

1959. Loaded coal wagons descend a self-acting incline on the Hetton Colliery Railway between Warden Law and North Moor. This part of the line was through open countryside.

2003. The course of the Hetton Colliery Railway incline can be seen beside the left-hand line of trees in the top of the photograph. Its route is now bisected by the A19. The former fields are now occupied by the Doxford International Business Park, one of the region's main centres of employment and site of the headquarters of several of Wearside's leading companies.

Sixty Years of Change

By 2003 Sunderland had probably undergone more changes since 1945 than any other city in the country. Shipbuilding and coal, the area's two biggest sources of employment, have disappeared along with most of the historic industries. Only glassmaking remains as a link with the sources of the great growth of the 19th century.

While the city has lost its historic industries it has established itself as a major centre for new sources of employment. Nissan, Europe's most successful car plant, and the Doxford International Business Park, with its call centres and administrative offices, are outstanding examples of the city's new economic base.

Another is the University, now a major employer as well as attracting a significant number of students from around Britain and from abroad to Sunderland. The city has also developed in other ways unforeseen in 1945. Several of its cultural and leisure facilities are now of regional significance.

There are still concerns about poor health and lack of educational achievement in particular parts of the city; these are of course the same problems that affect many similar urban areas. The standard of

housing, the major problem facing in the Council in the 1940s, has, however, vastly improved.

Sunderland is a very different place in 2003 from 1945 and its people have lived through 60 years of massive changes. They can be proud of the city's substantial recent achievements as well as of its past history.

The staff of Leighton, one of the companies at the forefront of new technology and communication, working in their office at Doxford International. Success in this field is as important for Sunderland today as shipbuilding once was.

Appendices

Appendix 1
Sunderland's Population from Census Returns

1931	185,824
1941	No Census
1951	181, 524
1961	189,686
1971	212,995
1981	294,894
1991	289,090
2001	280,807

The municipal boundaries were slightly extended in 1951 to take in part of Sunderland Rural District and in 1967 to include the remainder of the Rural District and the South Bents areas of Whitburn. The new Borough in 1974 comprised the areas of the County Borough and Hetton, Houghton-le-Spring and Washington Urban Districts and Burdon and Warden Law Parishes.

Appendix 2
Mayors of Sunderland

Elected

County Borough of Sunderland

November 1944	John Young (Mod)
November 1945	Joshua Ritson (Lab)
November 1946	Miles Walton (Lab)
November 1947	Eden Johnson (Lab)
May 1949	Jack Cohen (Lab)
May 1950	George Morgan (Lab)
May 1951	William Harvey (Lab)
May 1952	Arthur Suddick (Lab)
May 1953	McGregor English (Lab)
May 1954	Jane Huggins (Lab)
May 1955	Edith Blacklock (Lab)
May 1956	Thomas Cavanagh (Lab)
May 1957	Joseph Hoy (Lab)
May 1958	Edwin Wales (Lab)
May 1959	Nicholas Allison (Lab)
May 1960	Joseph Tweddle (Lab)
May 1961	Kitty Cohen (Lab)
May 1962	Richard Weston (Lab)
May 1963	Jane Hedley (Lab)
May 1964	Robert Wilkinson (Lab)
May 1965	Albert Watson (Lab)
May 1966	Fred Young (Lab)
May 1967	Norman Waters (Con)
May 1968	John Wilkinson (Con) *died*

February 1969	Mary Miller (Con)
May 1969	Mary Miller (Con)
May 1970	William Stephenson (Con)
May 1971	William Martin (Con)
May 1972	Leslie Watson (Lab)
May 1973	George Park (Lab)

Borough of Sunderland

May 1974	Arnold Burgham (Lab)
May 1975	Mary Porter (Lab)
May 1976	Charles Slater (Lab)
May 1977	Thomas Bridges (Lab)
May 1978	Arnold Lumley (Lab)
May 1979	Edward Weirs (Lab) *died*
September 1979	Leonard Harper (Lab)
May 1980	Leonard Harper (Lab)
May 1981	Thomas Finnigan (Lab)
May 1982	Joseph Hall (Lab)
May 1983	Annie Pratt (Lab)
May 1984	George Elliot (Lab)
May 1985	Ralph Baxter (Lab)
May 1986	Thomas Scott (Lab)
May 1987	John Mawston (Lab)
May 1988	Leslie Mann (Lab)
May 1989	Robert Kirby (Lab)
May 1990	Andrew Myers (Lab)
May 1991	David Thompson (Lab)

City of Sunderland

May 1992	William Craddock (Lab)
May 1993	Bryan Charlton (Lab)
May 1994	Denis Whalen (Lab)
May 1995	Eric Bramfitt (Lab)
May 1996	Ian Galbraith (Lab)
May 1997	Gowan Scott (Lab)
May 1998	Walter Scott (Lab)
May 1999	Ross Wares (Lab)
May 2000	Brian Dodds (Lab)
May 2001	Kenneth Murray (Lab)
May 2002	Peter Gibson (Lab)
May 2003	Juliana Heron (Lab)

Appendix 3
Town Clerks/Chief Executives

1932–1962	George McIntire
1962–1969	James Storey
1970–1973	James Gardner
1973–1980	Louis Bloom
1980–1993	Geoffrey Key
1993–2003	Colin Sinclair

Appendix 4
Members of Parliament whose constituencies included parts of the Sunderland local authority area:

General Election	*Sunderland*	
1945	Fred Willey (Lab)	
	Richard Ewart (Lab)	
	Sunderland North	*Sunderland South*
1950	Fred Willey (Lab)	Richard Ewart (Lab)
1951	Fred Willey (Lab)	Richard Ewart (Lab) *died*
1952 by-election		Paul Williams (Con)
1955	Fred Willey (Lab)	Paul Williams (Con)
1959	Fred Willey (Lab)	Paul Williams (Con)
1964	Fred Willey (Lab)	Gordon Bagier (Lab)
1966	Fred Willey (Lab)	Gordon Bagier (Lab)
1970	Fred Willey (Lab)	Gordon Bagier (Lab)
Feb 1974	Fred Willey (Lab)	Gordon Bagier (Lab)
Oct 1974	Fred Willey (Lab)	Gordon Bagier (Lab)
1979	Fred Willey (Lab)	Gordon Bagier (Lab)
1983	Bob Clay (Lab)	Gordon Bagier (Lab)
1987	Bob Clay (Lab)	Chris Mullin (Lab)
1992	Bill Etherington (Lab)	Chris Mullin (Lab)
1997	Bill Etherington (Lab)	Chris Mullin (Lab)
2001	Bill Etherington (Lab)	Chris Mullin (Lab)
	Houghton-le-Spring	*Chester-le-Street*
Oct 1974	Tom Urwin (Lab)	Giles Radice (Lab)
1979	Tom Urwin (Lab)	Giles Radice (Lab)
	Houghton and Washington	
1983	Roland Boyes (Lab)	
1987	Roland Boyes (Lab)	
1992	Roland Boyes (Lab)	
		Gateshead East and Washington West
1997	Fraser Kemp (Lab)	Joyce Quin (Lab)
2001	Fraser Kemp (Lab)	Joyce Quin (Lab)

Bibliography

Adie, Kate *The Kindness of Strangers* Headline, 2002.

Anderson, Albert *The Dream Palaces of Sunderland* Mercia Cinema Society, 1982.

Baker, John C. and Others *Pyrex Sixty Years of Design*, Tyne and Wear County Council Museums, 1983.

Baker, John C. *Sunderland Pottery* Tyne and Wear County Council Museums, 1984.

Bowling, Helen G. *Some Chapters on the History of Sunderland* Privately Published, 1969.

Brett, Alan *Sunderland Public Houses* Black Cat, 2003.

City Hospitals Sunderland NHS Trust *Annual Report 2002/2003.*

Clarke, J.F. *Building Ships on the North East Coast Vol. 2* Bewick Press, 1997.

Copland, Dick *Lesson in Class* TUPS Books, 1998.

Corfe Tom *Sunderland, a Short History* Frank Graham, 1973.

Corfe, Tom and Geoffrey Milburn *Buildings and Beliefs* Wearside Historic Churches Group, 1994.

County Borough of Sunderland *Sunderland Municipal Handbook*, 1966.

Curtis, Philip *Sunderland A Century of Shopping* The People's History, 1999.

Dennis, Norman *People and Planning* Faber and Faber, 1970.
Public Participation and Planners' Blight Faber and Faber, 1972.

Gibson, Peter *Southwick-on-Wear Vol. 4*, Southwick Publications, 1996.

Dodds, Glen Lyndon *A History of Sunderland* Albion Press, 1995.

Holley, Stephen *Quicker By Quango: the History of Washington New Town 1964–1983* Publication for Companies, 1983.

Hopkins, Gordon *The Moving Staircase: Sunderland 1939–72* Wearside Press, 1972.

Hughes, David *A Journey to Remember* County Durham Books, 2000.

Jessop, L. and N.T. Sinclair *Sunderland Museum* Tyne and Wear Museums, 1996.

Kirtley, Mel *Sunderland in the Sixties* Wearside Books, 1995.
Sunderland in the Fifties Wearside Books, 1998.

Maclaghan, J.B. *Report on School Health, Public Health and Port Health Services of the Borough* County Borough of Sunderland, 1948 and 1955.

Martin, Gareth (Ed) *Memories of Sunderland* True North Books, 1998.

Martin, Phil *The Tom Cowie Story* James & James, 1988.

Milburn, Geoffrey E., Stuart T. Miller and Others *Sunderland River, Town and People* Borough of Sunderland, 1988.

Mitchell, Andrew (Ed) *More Memories of Sunderland* True North Books, 2001.

Nicholson, Sir Paul *Brewer at Bay* The Memoir Club, 2003.

Roberton, Carol, Phil Hall and Others *Millennium Sunderland* (12 parts) *Sunderland Echo*, 1999.

Robson, B.T. *Urban Analysis: A study of City structures with special reference to Sunderland* Cambridge, 1969.

Sayers, Audrey B. *Sunderland Church High School for Girls* Privately Published, 1984.

Sinclair, Helen M. *Cycle Clips* Tyne and Wear County Council Museums, 1985.

Sinclair, Neil T. *The River Wear* Tyne and Wear County Council Museums, 1984.

Railways of Sunderland Tyne and Wear Museums Service, 1986.

Smith, J.W. and T.S. Holden *Where Ships Are Born* Thomas Reed, 1946.

Staddon, S.A. *The Tramways of Sunderland* Sunderland Echo, 1991.

Sunderland Area Hospital Committee *Report 1950–1951.*

Sunderland City Challenge *Official Guide*, 1995.

Sunderland Health Authority *Director of Public Health Annual Report, 2000–2002.*

Tyne and Wear Development Corporation *Regeneration Statement, 1998.*

A Vision for the Future, 1989.

Wayman, David *Sunderland Corporation Buses* North East Press, 1997.

Wilson, Alisdair R. (Ed) *Football Under the Skin* Tyne and Wear Museums Service, 1988.

Wilson, Martyn and Karen Speak *Coles 100 Years* Coles, 1978.

Yearnshire, John *Back on the Borough Beat* John Yearnshire, 1987.

Index

159